THE WAY OUT

THE WAY OUT

CHOICES

GILBERT M. GRIÑIE

STONEWALL PRESS
PAVING YOUR WAY TO SUCCESS

The Way Out
Copyright © 2018 by Gilbert Griñie. All rights reserved.

No part of this publication may be reproduced, stored in a retrieval system or transmitted in any way by any means, electronic, mechanical, photocopy, recording or otherwise without the prior permission of the author except as provided by USA copyright law.

The opinions expressed by the author are not necessarily those of Stonewall Press.

Published in the United States of America

ISBN: 978-1-64460-082-5 (*sc*)
       978-1-64460-081-8 (*e*)

Library of Congress Control Number: 2018966505

Stonewall Press books may be ordered through booksellers or by contacting:

Stonewall Press
4800 Hampden Lane, Suite 200
Bethesda, MD 20814 USA
www.stonewallpress.com
1-888-334-0980
orders@stonewallpress.com

Memoirs (Biography/Autobiography)
19.01.19

I dedicate this thesis to the most important person in my life Gloria Griñie, my wife. You are the backbone of our marriage. Your patience, love, and courage helped me make that one hundred and eighty degrees turn in my life and steered me in the right direction. I want to thank my kids and grandkids for supporting and encouraging both of us to have patience. The love that I have for you is infinite and priceless, and I look forward to the day when we can spend more quality time together.

Contents

Preface 11
Acknowledgements 13
The Way Out 15

Chapter 1   Introduction.. 17

                Scope of Problem.. 19
                Statement of Problem 20
                Purpose of Study 21
                Assumptions of the Study.................................... 22
                Questions to Be Answered 22
                Theorticacal Framework....................................... 23
                Definitions of Terms... 25
                Thesis Structure 27

Chapter 2   Review of the Literature History
                of Ethnic Gangs in the United States................... 29

                Introduction... 29
                Irish Gangs in New York 31
                Chinese Gangs in New York City......................... 33
                Italian Gangs in New York 34

	Ethnic Gangs in Chicago	38
	African American Gangs	40
	Ethnic Gangs in Los Angeles	43
	Chicano/Latino Gangs in Los Angeles	44
	1943 Race Riots and Pachuco Gangs	46
	Gang Structure and Activities from the 1940s to the Present	47
	Gang Characteristic	48
	Youth Gang Structure	51
Chapter 3	Methodology	55
	Limitations	58
Chapter 4	Mexican-American Heritage in the Southwest, Immigration Patterns, and Chicano/Latino Gangs in the City and County of Los Angeles	59
	Mexican Settlement of the Southwest: 1840 to Present	59
	Chicano/Latinos Account for an Increasing Percentage in the U.S. Population	60
	A Brief History of Mexican Settlement of the Southwest and Los Angeles	66
	Barrios in Los Angeles	69
	Immigration Patterns Related to Economics and Political Factors	71
	Repatriation Policy	74
	World War II and the Bracero Program	75
	Factors Influencing the Increase of Political Activity by Chicanos/Latinos in Los Angeles County	77

	Early Chicano/Latino Gangs 78
	Pachuco Gangs 80
	The Effect of World War II 81
	The Increase in Numbers of Gangs and Gang Violence...................................... 83

Chapter 5	Case Studies in the Form of Oral Interviews........ 87
	Oral Interview #1 88
	Oral Interview #2 106

Chapter 6	Summary, Solutions, and Suggestions Proposed for Further Research and Conclusion 121
	Suggestions for Further Research 125
	Solutions.. 126
	Prevention.. 128
	Conclusion... 129

References.. 131

Appendix A	"Set A" Questions for Non-Gang Members 139
Appendix B	"Set B" Questions for Gang and Retired Gang Members................................... 141

Article from Sun-News Newspaper By Rebecca Johns
    Sun-News Reporter.. 145

Photo Section 153

Preface
By Gloria, Melissa, Ronnie, Sonya Griñie

VIOLENCE, GANG ASSOCIATION & mayhem has been an unfortunate side effect of immigrants who arrived to America since the 1820's, beginning with the arrival of Irish immigrants. What is so tragic is that almost 190 years later, after a colossal invasion of Asian, Italian and Latino immigrants, our society has yet to tackle this concern in a powerful manner.

In his book, Gilbert G. Griñie explores the development of gangs of ethnicity in the United States and clears up frequently accepted misunderstandings about gang members which include oral interviews with former members of gangs from two different Chicano/Latino gangs. Gilbert G. Griñie enlightens on external factors that do contribute to adolescents becoming gang members, such as poverty-stricken upbringings and lack of work. It also goes toward the role of parents & their lack of parenting skills. "Youth whose families are not meeting their emotional needs turn to gangs as surrogate families where they find approval."

Griñie also explains that adolescents reach out to gangs out of "a need for protection from other gangs, the need to find personal identity, and the need to have stability and structure in their lives."

According to Gilbert M. Griñie's studies, the literature in relation to the expansion of gangs in the United States disclose that "ethnic gangs were an essential part of the absorption process of immigrants and their offspring into the social, political and economic realms of society"; especially because it's difficult to "adapt to a society that offers little or no support in the process". Understanding the causes that motivate adolescents to be part of a gang can inform intervention strategies.

Gilbert M. Griñie takes a step further and offers specific steps to confront and attack the problem, such as transferring justice dollars to finance education, housing, child care, healthcare, jobs and careers, also to include effective suppression strategies by law enforcement and create special education programs for K-12 students who are at risk.

Gilbert M. Griñie's book comes at a critical time in our history; a time when society can no longer afford to ignore, disregard or neglect this issue that is affecting our lives on a daily basis.

Acknowledgements

IT HAS BEEN A long and tough journey for me both as an undergraduate and as graduate student here at California State University, Los Angeles. Shortly before my transfer to CSULA, I was involved in an industrial accident the results of which confronted me with many challenges. The severity of the injury made me question whether I would even graduate.

First, I would like to thank the Department of Administration and Counseling for their support and guidance in helping me reach my goal. I want to give a very special thanks to Dr. Martin Brodwin who took me under his wing and encouraged me to pursue a Master's degree in Counseling.

I am very grateful to the individuals who have assisted me in the completion of this thesis. I would like to thank Dr. Marcel Soriano for taking his position as the Chair for this committee. Dr. Pauline Mercado for her assistance and time she has given in the completion of this thesis. Many thanks go to Dr. Richard T. Rodriguez for coming on board at such a late stage of this research and guiding me in the structure of this thesis. I also thank the rest of the members from the different communities within the county of Los Angeles, Gilbert Sanchez, Donald Irving, Mike Garcia, Claudia Padilla, Tim Rodriguez, Alex Sanchez, Waldo Rodriguez, as well as Victor Bono, Silva Beltran, Luis Viscarra, Carlos Marchena, and Beverly Keefe for their assistance on this project.

Finally, this study would have taken me a lot longer to complete without the assistance of Dr. Sharon Johnson who with her patience and caring spirit made it possible. Thank you, Dr. Johnson, for your assistance and guidance.

The Way Out
By Gilbert M. Griñie

THIS RESEARCH PRESENTS AN historical perspective of ethnic gangs in the United States, specifically of Chicano/Latino gangs in the city and county of Los Angeles. A review of the historical literature about ethnic gangs in the United States is the platform from which this work builds. The researcher presents information about Chicano/Latino gangs gained through personal interviews with active gang members, retired gang members, and individuals in non-profit organizations that address gang violence. Two interviews are presented in their entirety in Chapter Four. The study describes factors influencing ethnic gang formation and sheds light on the reasons why Chicano/Latino youth join violent gangs.

This research is further designed to provide an understanding of how the social problem of violence and gang activity presents a major challenge for all ethno-cultural groups within communities in Los Angeles. Street gangs have existed in the County of Los Angeles since the turn of the twentieth century. If society is to try to reduce and control gangs and the violence associated with gangs, we must invest in public safety by relocating justice dollars to finance education, housing, healthcare, and jobs. We must also include suppression by law enforcement and education programs aimed at K-12 school students. Although this researcher suggests further research, proposed solutions are proposed in this thesis.

Chapter 1

Introduction

"Since the retirement of former Los Angeles Police Chief Daryl Gates, there is a lot to say about everything that has to do with gang members. The portrayal of all gang members has misled the public to believe that all gang members as bad, and portraying that they should be locked up for the safety of the communities. Gang members are people, just as you and me, and they need someone to understand them and take them under their wing and help them realize that education is the most powerful tool they will need to succeed in life. They have feelings and fears, and they get scared to go out at night just like anybody else."

– Silva Beltran,
Executive Director, Homies Unidos.

THIS THESIS IS DESIGNED to give the reader an understanding of how the social problem of violence and gang activity presents a major challenge for all ethno-cultural groups within communities throughout Los Angeles. Research findings suggest that the level of violence has escalated over the past years to a point that communities feel significantly threatened (Howell, Krisberg, Hawkings & Wilson, 1995). However, statistics show that by the end of December 2003, the latest data posted on the LAPD website (www.lapd.org), gang related homicides were down 21.6% from a year ago (LAPD website, 2003). Street gangs have existed in the county of Los Angeles since the 1940s. Gangs contribute to criminal problems within the urban settings of Los Angeles and within our schools. School disruptions by gang members interfere with teaching, and learning remains a significant problem for these students in their quest for education (Chavez, 2001). According to Diego Vigil (2000), the Los Angeles area tops the list with approximately 8,000 gangs and 200,000 gang members. Historically, both social and economic factors have contributed to the origin of gangs.

Most gang related information comes from law enforcement agencies, detention facilities, and prisons; data from these sources reflect a lack of reporting standardization. According to a survey conducted by the Office of Juvenile Justice, Delinquency, and Prevention (OJJDP), there is wide variation in the quality of data reported (Juvenile Justice Clearinghouse, 1995). Therefore, data on gang activities remains incomplete and often inaccurate. However, the prevalence of criminal behavior in youth and the problems this presents to the community are real.

Gang participation has a long history among young males (although Miranda, 2004, for a study of girl gangs) within poor communities in U.S. history. Immigrants find it especially difficult to adapt to a society that offers little or no support in the process. The failure to becoming acculturated and living in low-income communities contribute to the probability of young males joining gangs. Those who join gangs share many common personality traits acknowledged as risk factors. These risk factors according to Greenan, S., Britz, M., Rush, J., and Barker, T. (2000) are the need for protection from other gangs, the need to find personal identity, and the need to have stability and structure in their lives. Furthermore, research shows that gang members could have been exposed to alcohol or drug abuse, may feel rejected, may do badly in school, and may live in a single parent family setting where guidance and mentorship is lacking (Gedatus, 2000).

Education, in contrast to gangs, is a key to maintaining a competitive society in the 21st century. The educational system in California is at odds with educating at-risk youth or students who are underrepresented. Many public schools have become mere depositories for the children of poor working families. Children are more at-risk when they attend schools where drug use is endemic, and where the threat of violence is inevitable. Achievement opportunities and social learning that were not provided in childhood are sought through gang membership; this is viewed as an alternative to what was not offered in the home or school environment (Spergel, 1992). To reach at-risk youth, more attention should be given to the type of services provided by our schools and communities. Professionals such as social workers, working as a team in the community with at-risk children and youth, would enhance the potential for success and possible avoidance of gang affiliation (Adler, Hocevar, & Ovando, 1984). This as an alternative could provide students opportunities to build self-esteem at a time when it is crucial to human development. Even though today's educational system has failed to address the needs of at-risk youth, with proper improvements educational reform can function to reduce gang involvement.

Scope of Problem

Research demonstrates that observational learning also known as imitation or modeling is significantly correlated with a person's tendency to engage in aggressive behavior. Albert Bandura reported that individuals who live in high crime areas are more likely to act violently then those who dwell in low-crime areas (Bandura, 1976: 207). The lack of parental interface and guidance increases the risk for aggression, especially among young males in communities with limited resources (Brownstein, 2000).

Living in a poor neighborhood, where youth violence impacts not only individuals but families who live in fear, puts youth at an elevated probability for joining gangs (Howell, 1998). For example, Los Angeles is home to the largest population of Salvadorans outside San Salvador and the largest population of Mexicans outside of Mexico (Vigil, 2002, Hamilton and Chinchilla, 2001). Chicano/Latino gangs look down on and attack the Salvadoran immigrants and other Central Americans; and Mexican immigrants frequently voice resentment of Latinos. "Mexican domination" is noted everywhere from the workplace to the school system. Central Americans express this domination in the following ways, "Mexicans think they own Los Angeles" (Hamilton and Chinchilla, 2001: p. 57). Safeguard from this violence has become a necessity for survival, and therefore ethnic groups they band together: to provide themselves with protection.

Statement of Problem

It is important to examine the relationships that exist between families in low-income neighborhoods and the resources made available to them. Gang life is traditional to the Chicano/Latino living in predominantly Chicano/Latino neighborhoods. It is a subculture that an inmost circle is an accepted pattern of life in the neighborhood, or barrio. Identified family variables, including poverty, absence of biological parents, and limited parental supervision may increase the probability of gang membership. Many gang members follow in the footsteps of their parents or family members (such as brothers, uncles, aunts, cousins) who, at one time, were themselves gang members. Others join gangs for a variety of reasons, including physical protection, peer pressure, profit, adventure, or to belong to the subcommunity. In Los Angeles, criminal youth enterprises have become permanent fixtures. The criminal gang has perhaps become one of the more dangerous and enduring institutions of our times, given the fact of its stubbornness in surviving changing social and economic conditions (see Luis Rodriguez, Always Running). Gangs in Los Angeles were evident as early as the 1940s (Haskins, 1974). Their presence is still highlighted in today's media as well as in scholarly literature. The existence of gangs in Los Angeles is well documented throughout the 20th century and continues into the 21st century (Adler, P., Hocevar, D., & Ovando, C. (1984); Spergel, I. A. (1992); Vigil, D. J. (2000).

While gangs as a subculture have remained somewhat unwavering in the community of Los Angeles, they have changed in the level to which they have become complex, aggressive, and organized. It has been suggested that not only in Los Angeles, but throughout the United States, communities have been plagued by the continued growth and strengthening of delinquent and/or criminal countercultures for the past several years (Campbell 1987; Chin 1990; Fagan 1990; Maxson and Klein 1990, Kontos, Barrios, and Brotuertan, 2003).

Crime figures suggest that today's gangs create a more acute crime problem than in the past. Literature suggests that young people whose families are not meeting their emotional needs turn to gangs as surrogate families where they find approval. Communal problems linked to gang activity are poverty, racial bias, and the breakdown of the nuclear family (Gale Encyclopedia of Childhood & Adolescents, 1998).

Purpose of Study

The study of history in schools and universities often seems to amount to little more than rote learning about proceedings, battles, and personalities. H. G. Wells said that the narrow teaching of history in our school days was mainly "an uninspiring and partially forgotten list of national kings and presidents" (Awake, 1984, p. 4).

The purpose of this study is to provide an historical perspective on the formation of Chicano/Latino gangs in Los Angeles

County, and to explore the impact of past family violence, and drug trafficking within the communities of the Los Angeles. An understanding family conditions and behaviors that motivate young males to join gangs can provide direction for intervention so that social workers can better understand the dynamics of this client population. Research on family violence and drug trafficking correlated with young male gang involvement can be used to educate social agencies as well as the community about the complexity of working with this population.

Assumptions of the Study

1. It was assumed that all the information gathered would be pertinent to this study.
2. It was assumed by the researcher that the questions asked in the interview would be pertinent to this study and that all respondents would give information valuable to the study.
3. It was assumed that the questions asked in the interviews would be easy for the respondents to answer, and that their responses would be given honestly and without deception.
4. Lastly, it was assumed that the information from the two audiotaped case studies would be honestly given and that it would be of value to this study, since it was given by persons who are now assets to the community and dedicated their lives to working with the communities they grew up in as intervention specialists.

Questions to Be Answered

1. Do young males who get involved in gangs report a history of violence and narcotic trafficking?
2. How can intervention and prevention stop gang involvement from undercutting efforts at civic renewal?

3. Is childhood abuse (emotional, physical neglect, sexual abuse and witnessing domestic violence) a contributing factor that influences young males to join gangs?

Theorticacal Framework

Families, communities, and society in general usually motivate persons to behave in socially standard ways. However, social learning theory says that individuals obtain certain behavioral attitudes by social learning, in this case from gang peers and criminal behavior. The social learning theory is the behavior theory most relevant to criminology, and I will expand upon in this thesis. Albert Bandura believed that aggression is learned through a process called behavioral modeling. He believed that individuals do not actually inherit violent tendencies, but that they are the result of modeling, which consist of three principles (Bandura, 1976: p 204). First is association or classical conditioning, second is operant conditioning, and third is modeling. Examples of each principle are; the first is association or classical conditioning, which consist of learning when two events repeatedly occur close together in time. The second in operant conditioning, humans and animals learn to behave in certain ways because of receiving reward-any satisfying consequences-whenever they do so. The third known as modeling, individuals learn responses simply by observing other individuals and repeating their behaviors.

Gang members who come from homes where there is limited nurturing by parental figures are likely to show signs of poor self-esteem and, in many cases, cause problems in the classroom. Alternatives to gang programs are needed in addition to counseling, such as job training, jobs, and educational support to help at-risk youth lead more positive creative lives (Spergel, 1992). Trustworthiness, respect, responsibility, fairness, caring, and citizenship are values that comprise a core ethics that needs to be taught in the home, and be reinforced within in the classroom

(Josephson Institute, 2000). These values serve as a guide for individuals in making appropriate decisions.

Studies of gang structure and activities, initiated the effort to develop an adequate theory, which would explain the creation of gangs. *The Gang*, (Bloch, 1958), and *Delinquency and Opportunity* (Cloward & Ohin, 1960) are two studies which consider theoretical aspects of gang behavior. One theory holds that delinquent subcultures are a response to a conflict in cultural codes, for example, the clash between lower and middle-class values, (Cloward & Ohin, 1960). Other theoreticians suggest that the gang is, in its roots, a specific reaction to the keen stresses of adolescence, and disagree that the gang originates in the conflict between the aspirations of lower class youth and their prospect of fulfilling those aspirations by lawful means.

In her study of three gangs in the city and county of Los Angeles, (Moore, 1978) proposes a theory not unlike that of Cloward and Ohlin. She attributes the construction and stability of the modern Chicano/Latino gang in Los Angeles to the tripartite nature of the economic opportunity structure and its impact on gang members. The members find it impossible to enter the labor market and, therefore, resort to a strategy to make ends meet either from income available through government programs or through illegal activities, such as the drug trade.

These theories describe recurrent themes in the literature on gangs, and should not be considered incompatible. Nor do these theories or interpretations of the gang exhaust the list of factors influential in the configuration of gangs. McWilliams (1949), for instance, in his insightful treatment of the 1943 race riots in Los Angeles, speaks of the "iron curtain" surrounding East Los Angeles, effectively excluding Chicano/Latino youth from productive activities available to their Anglo counterparts. Howard Erlanger (1982) expands on a similar theme when he speaks of the marginal position of Chicano/Latino youth in the City and County of Los Angeles. Gang members are alienated from their cultural roots as well as cut off from the dominant society as well.

Definitions of Terms

For this study, the following terms are provided:

- Anglo: Any person of the "White" northern European race, specifically Anglo-Saxon or Germanic/Gaelic. More commonly specified as "any Caucasian person in the United States who is not Chicano/Latino.
- Barrio: Spanish term for neighborhood, used by gang members to refer to their "gang" or "neighborhood."
- Bracero: A contracted Mexican laborer who was admitted working in the United States under the Bracero program that began in the 1940s and ended in December 1964.
- Chicano/Latino: For this study, the term Chicano/Latino will be used to identify the Mexican, Mexican-American, and others having a Spanish-speaking ancestry, such as Salvadorans and any culture of Latino descent.
- Family: a group of people who live together and are related to each other by marriage, blood, or adoption.
- Gang Member: A person who declares himself or herself to be a member of a specific gang whose allegiance to the group is expressed in verbal statements and specific behaviors. Members identify themselves through their dress, graffiti writing, language, and tattoos, which are used to express their territorial pride (Corson, 1981).
- Homeboy/Homegirl: A name used by members in the neighborhood to identify males or females in the neighborhood gang or group. Members identify themselves as homeboys/homegirls to indicate they "belong" to a specific neighborhood with their friends.
- Juvenile: The term denotes a young person under the legal age of 18 years.

- Machismo: "Machismo" comes from the root word "macho" which can translate simply as "male." It means having courage, not backing down or showing any signs of weakness, being ready to fight, and being dominant.
- Mexican-American: The traditional term employed to identify the American citizen of Mexican ancestry.
- Mexican-National: A native-born citizen of Mexico.
- Palabra: A power figure that is respected by the gang in the barrio.
- Retired Gang Member: A person who at one time was part of a gang but no longer participates in any gang activity.
- Veterano: Spanish term for veteran, meaning a former gang member who maintains communication with his/her gang, but who usually no longer participates in gang violence. To become a veterano, the gang member goes through a process of transformation, usually at the age of 22, from being a homeboy to becoming a veterano. Further, a veterano is one who is usually married and is often involved with drugs.
- Youth Gang: The following definition has been given by the Attorney General's Youth Gang Task Force in describing all gangs in California: "A youth gang is an organization of individuals between the ages of 14-24 years. It is loose knit, without structure, and the strongest or boldest member is usually the leader. The gang has a name, claims a territory or neighborhood, is involved in criminal activity, and its member's associate on a continuous basis. Their activities include violent assaults against other gangs, as well as committing crimes against the general population, (California, 1981, p. 3).
- Social Learning Theory: "A modern offshoot of behaviorism that places primary emphasis on how people learn social behaviors from one another, especially through social reinforcement and modeling" (Taylor, Peplau, and Seadrs, 2000).

Thesis Structure

The remainder of this is comprised of five more chapters.

Chapter 2, "Overview of the Development of Ethnic Gangs and of Chicano/Latino Gangs": explores the general development of ethnic gangs in America, the development of Chicano/Latino gangs in Los Angeles within the City and County of Los Angeles, and describes the common characteristics of these gangs.

Chapter 3, "Methodology," looks at the methodology and procedures used to collect the data and the limitations of this research.

Chapter 4, "Chicano/Latino Heritage in the Southwest, Immigration Patterns, Chicanos/Latinos account for an increasing percentage in the U.S. population, and Chicano/Latino Gangs within the City and County of Los Angeles," explores the development of Chicano/Latino settlements in the Southwest, the political changes that developed when the Southwest Territories were joined to the United States by treaty with Mexico, the rise of Chicano/ Latino population in the Southwest, the barrios of Los Angeles, and their growth and expansion into all parts of the County and City of Los Angeles, with the concomitant rise in Chicano/Latino gangs and gang violence.

Chapter 5, "Case Studies," includes two oral interviews with retired gang members from two Chicano/Latino gangs. These interviews demonstrate effectively what gangs are doing today. These case studies substantiate the activities and history of the gangs as well as illustrate the reasons why Chicano/Latino youth join gangs.

Chapter 6, "Summary, Conclusions, and Suggestions for Further Research," discusses the findings of this study concerning the many parallels among ethnic gangs. Solutions to the gang phenomenon are offered, the researcher also suggests areas where further study can be helpful in improving the understanding of gang behavior.

Chapter 2

Review of the Literature History of Ethnic Gangs in the United States

Introduction

GANGS IN LOS ANGELES have become a rising challenge within our communities where more and more adolescents are committing violent crimes. At the turn of the 21st century, gangs became a major concern of law enforcement within Los Angeles and it is surrounding communities. Violence cuts short the lives of many individuals either by death or incarceration across the county of Los Angeles each year, and damages the lives of many more. It knows no boundaries of geography, race, age, and income. The purpose of this investigation is to look at variables that result in gang involvement.

This chapter presents a review of the overall literature on gangs throughout history in the United States and the literature on Chicano/Latino gangs in the City and County of Los Angeles. The importance of this literature is to formulate an historical perspective on the formation of gangs in cultural groups such as Irish, Italians, Chinese, and Chicanos/Latinos. Therefore, the literature cited will show the resemblance of socioeconomic patterns of gangs among other cultures in relation to the growth of Hispanic gangs in Los Angeles County. For an understanding of the incidence of youth gangs, a survey of the literature which conveys some hypothetical proposals for youth gangs is included. As a decisive point, the universal the general arrangement and distinctiveness of modern-day youth gangs is presented.

The literature in relation to the growth of gangs in the ethnic communities in the United States reveals that ethnic gangs were an essential part of the absorption process of immigrants and their offspring into the social, political, and economic realms of society (Haskins, 1974; Thrasher, 1963). For example, Haskins (1974) traces gang-like behavior of young people from the colonial era to the present. He shows that many European immigrants came to America and settled in New York City, in hopes of finding an improved life. Most of those were poor and settled in destitute sections of the city where previous immigrants from their native country already resided. This migration procedure resulted in cultural communities of Irish (1820s-1830s), Italian (1880s-1890s), and Chinese (1880s-1910) immigrants.

Gangs in Los Angeles are not a new or current phenomenon. They can be traced back to the 1920s, and initially were formed as a means of self-preservation and as social clubs. According to Thrasher, "By the 1920s, more than 1,300 gangs had been reported in the city of Chicago; about this time, gangs began to form and have subsistence in Los Angeles, CA" (Vigil, 2002, p. 5).

There is no doubt that life for a young person in Los Angeles is more violent today than ever before. Within both the African American and Chicano/Latino, community's gang activity has become urbanized and flourishes. According to Wiener (1999), aggression is part of everyday life, and communities prefer to lean towards it rather than to prevent it. Rather than looking at gang violence as an isolated, observable fact, society needs to look at the motives of all forms of violence and abuses. It is much easier to target one group and label it "the problem" without looking at the contributing factors. Economic and social factors, which contribute to it, in addition to examining, all form of violence that occur in the communities.

Irish Gangs in New York

The mass of Irish immigrants in the 1820s and 1830s was largely received by the State of New York. Settling in the Five Point District of New York City, most of the Irish immigrants were poor. "The only neighborhood that would take them was the Five Points District," an area which "derived its name from the intersection of five streets, Anthony, Orange, Cross, Little, and Mulberry [today, Worth, Baxter, Park, and Mulberry Streets]" (Haskins, 1974, p. 24). This also included Paradise Square. Every livable space had been taken over by the Irish in this area. The Irish, considered there new as home "a land of cold and hunger and squalidness, of discrimination worse than they had known in their native land" (Haskins, 1974, p. 24). Haskins found that unlawful behavior among the Irish immigrants of the Five Points District grew as they engaged in robberies, burglaries, homicides, and prostitution.

The Irish in New York formed "the first true New York street gangs" according to Haskins (1974). This first gang was formed under the leadership of Edward Coleman in 1826, in the Five Points District. The organization of the gang took place in the back of Rosanna Peer's grocery store, which the gang used as a front. Adopting the name Forty Thieves the gang organized with a definite knowledge of leadership, which kept the gang together for many years. From his control center, Coleman "dispatched the gang members to rob, murder or beat any well-dressed man or law enforcement officer foolish enough to enter the district" (Haskins, 1974, p.26).

Other organized gangs began to appear in Paradise Square and at the Bowery a few years later. Youth gangs, such as the Roach

Guards, the Plug Uglies, the Bowery Boys, and a gang called the Dead Rabbits were terrorizing the community. Gang members engaged in fighting, hung out at beer gardens, and involved themselves in other criminal behavior. Haskins (1974) found that gangs "fought over territory just as gangs fight over 'turf' in the twentieth century" (p. 28). Gangs that would fight one another in Paradise Square and the Five Points District, would come together to fight gangs from other areas. For example, Haskins states: "In Paradise Square, although the Roach Guards and Dead Rabbits constantly fought each other, they forgot their differences when facing the Bowery gangs and fought side by side" (p. 28).

The battles would last two to three days in endless melees of beatings, disfigurement, and murder between gangs of the Paradise Square and those of the Bowery. Haskins notes that the battled were of such a degree that the government troops had to be called to help control the streets: The police were sometimes able to quell the fray—at considerable physical risk. Any officer caught by gangs faced beating, torture, maiming, or even death. Often, they were forced to ask the assistance of the National Guard and the regular Army. Regiments of soldiers in full battle dress marching through the streets to the scene of a gang melee, were not an uncommon sight in New York. Generally, they had no trouble dispersing the gangs. (p. 29) Violence among gangs is not 20th century phenomenon since, in the post-colonial period, gangs engaged in it repeatedly. Weapons that were used during that period, were pistols, muskets, knives, brickbats, bludgeons, brass knuckles, ice picks, etc. Women fought on the outskirts of the battles, ready to give medical aid, to supply ammunition, and sometimes even jump into the fray, (Haskins, 1974). Afterward, as the Irish moved to other cities, they would shape new gangs that paralleled the growth and behavior of the gangs in New York.

The number of juvenile gangs after the Civil War (1870-1890s) increased enormously and had their own offices and organizations, but were under the control of adult gangs, according to Haskins (1974). Haskins further states that: Juvenile gangs poured forth from all the poverty and slum pockets of the city, from neighborhoods with such descriptive names as Rotten Row, Poverty Lane, and Misery Row. The Nineteenth Street Gang and the Fourth Avenue Tunnel Gang were particularly notorious. Like their elders, they engaged in gang fights, maintained club houses, admired bravado and usually committed crimes only in groups. (p. 56) Involved with morphine, laudanum, and cocaine, gangs in the 1870s, '80s, '90s, were frequently drug users. These drugs gave the gang members the bravado and bravery to commit crimes. "Perhaps ninety percent of the [Hudson] Dusters were cocaine addicts, and when under the influence of the drug were very dangerous, for they were insensible to ordinary punishment, and were possessed of great, if artificial, bravery and ferocity." (Haskins, 1974, p. 51)

Chinese Gangs in New York City

In the era of industrialization America required cheap labor for all its new railroads and factories. Recruitment of Asians began in America in the 1880s to meet the demand for labor. As the Chinese arrived in New York, they settled in an area known as Chinatown. Chinatown, had previously been inhabited by Germans, and a few Irish. In 1880, there were 700 Chinese living in the area, and by 1910, there were between 10,000 and 15,000 (Haskins, 1974).

Upon arrival, "the Chinese formed clandestine networks, which first were mutual-aid societies whose membership depended on which province in China a person was from (Haskins, 1974, p. 58). However, as their numbers grew, these turned into aggressive groups, who were involved in scandalous behavior. The first Chinese to engage in unlawful behavior was Wah Kee, who used his grocery curio store in the Pell and Mott Streets area as a front for gambling and to provide opium smoking quarters (Haskins, 1974). By the mid-1890s, there were 200 gambling houses and as many opium dens operating in Chinatown.

In the early in 1900s, disagreements began among the Chinese because one gang would want to control Chinatown. The war between the Hip Sings and the On Leongs. As they would have competed for power to manage the unlawful operations, the aggression became so noticeable that the community started to become alarmed and the authorities had to intercede to bring peace between the two factions in 1906.

Chinatown was relatively peaceful until 1912 when a new leader, the Kim Lau Wui San, arose and declared war on the Hip Sings and the On Leongs (Haskins, 1974). It was now that both former factions united together to destroy the new forces which was intruding on their territory and declared war on them. With the new leader out of the way, the On Leongs and Hip Sings continued their success relative peace.

Italian Gangs in New York

The industrial growth of the 1880s in America resulted in the need for labor, which in turn opened the doors for new immigrants, especially the Italians, to enter America.

These new immigrants were like the Irish before them and the Chinese, mostly poor and uneducated (Garraty, 1979).

Italians who immigrated to America settled in the two major points of entry—New York City and New Orleans. They were plagued with the same tribulations of estrangement, discrimination, unemployment, congested housing. Haskins (1974) states was the norm for new immigrants of the 1870-1890s in New York City: "Perhaps the poor were poor not because of laziness or choice but because of the conditions in which they were forced to live, because of the tenements where there was not even room to breathe, because of the squalor, because of the oppression, because of the utter hopelessness that there could ever be any way out (pp. 51-52)."

As the Italians migrated from Sicily and Italy to the United States, they brought with them certain traditions of a secret criminal society known as the Camorra or Mafia. Persons involved in unlawful activity prearranged with others in their community to victimize the weaker and more susceptible. Traditionally, the Mafia committed crimes of extortion, robbery, family feuds, and kidnapping for ransom. Once established in the United States, their activities included drug trafficking, gambling, prostitution, and loan-sharking. Additionally, the Mafia operated legal businesses and had a strong influence in politics. Once recognized, the Mafia, also known as *La Cosa Nostra*, evolved into a national organization with a centralized structure. This structure consisted of a ruling body, or committee, which directed the activities of the various subdivisions referred to as "families," each of which had its own leader. According to Valachi (Maas, 1968), "the members of the family were frequently related to each other, they were initiated into the family through a ceremony, and each family had its own territory and its own type of illegal activity" (p. 351).

Within the history of crime, the Mafia was certainly unique and one of the most feared of all gangs. When the Mafia came to America it changed its dress and became more sophisticated. It was obvious that Mafia retaliation showed no compassion for sex or age. Retribution, many times, took the form of killing the youngest member of the family to enforce demands, however according to Maas 1968: "[The Mafia] did not invent organized crime nor did they introduce it to this country. When the Italian immigrants arrived in the late 19th century, they encountered an underworld primarily in the hands of the Irish and Jews that had been there before them." (p. 61)

In 1890, the Mafia attracted national attention when David C. Hennessey, Chief of Police in New Orleans, was murdered while trying to curb its activities. At that time, a group of Mafiosi had taken over the loading docks in New Orleans. Racketeering on the docks had taken place and no freight could be unloaded until a fixed tribute was paid to the Matranga Brothers. The dispute had begun when the Provenzano Brothers moved in on the territory of the Matranga Brothers. A series of brutal murders that took place weekly alarmed the city. Chief Hennessey, who investigated, had gradually pieced together the details, at which time he encountered the Mafia. According to Sondern (1959), "the murders, he discovered, had been the result of a typical Mafia feud between the Matrangas and the Provenzano Brothers who had tried to move in on their territory" (p. 59). Hennessey was killed after all the information was ready to be presented to the grand jury. The investigation of the murder of the chief revealed that "the existence of a secret organization known as the Mafia had been established without doubt" (p. 60).

The beginning of the twentieth century brought with it the use of extensive firearms used by gangs. The use of weapons became more sophisticated. Gangsters not only carried weapons, but used them in their wars against one another. There were brawls all over the place, and the use of guns brought terror to the public. "Yet, the public's apprehensions were not reassured until about 1910 when the police began to recognize and take into custody gangs with more consistent success. Gang members were lost when their leaders were captured and locked up. Police began to appear on the scene to protect property and to take patrolling matters into their own hands. Possession of a gun became a prison offence in 1911. Gang wars were common in 1913, but by 1916, many the major gangs had been smashed. Through 1909 and 1919, major cities began to establish police training programs to help deal with the problems of the cities. The police began to be tougher on gangs and their leaders. But, during the Prohibition Era that began one year after ratification of the 18th amendment crime emerged as a major social problem. In this era, organized crime and the gangs began to profit by bootlegging liquor. Chicago had an idiosyncratic problem because of the heavy demand for beer by its large foreign-born population: the large-scale operation of supplying beer resulted in killings between rival gangs for the complete control of the operation. According to Haskins (1974): Within two years, every gang in Chicago and New York and their surrounding suburbs was engaged in bootlegging as its major operation. Italian gangs, Polish gangs, Irish gangs, Jewish gangs—no gang bothered the others, and all got richer and richer. But after three years the gangs became greedy, and gang wars over control of bootlegging in various areas broke out often (p. 71).

Organized and heavily armed, the Mafia was ready to obliterate or assassinate anyone who got in its way. The automobile was an invention that helped advance the Mafia's sophistication in criminal behavior. With prohibition came new classes of crime and diverse types of criminals. Underworld empires flourished in most major cities. To create an empire based on beer and liquor, the automobile and machine gun were used as basic tools. The police were almost helpless to do anything about the rapidly rising crime rate, due to a shortage of police officers. In his book, Garraty (1979) wrote: While gangsters such as Alphonse (Scarface Al) Capone of Chicago were engaged in the liquor traffic, hijacking one another's shipments, gunning down their enemies in broad daylight, and bombing rival distilleries and warehouses without regard for passing innocent, they and their "organizations" existed before the Eighteenth Amendment and were engaged in many other illegal activities. (p. 628)

Throughout this era, there was an increase in the public's concern with law enforcement in America. Commissions were created by many communities to study the gang problem in hope of finding a remedy. During this decade, more than one hundred surveys into crime and the breakdown of policing were taken. Many gangland homicides happened, but there were no murder trials because there were no witnesses who would testify. The gangs had reached into politics to guarantee their survival, by this time.

President Hoover appointed a Commission on Law Observance and Enforcement on May 1929, charging it with investigating the entire field of crime and lawlessness in the United States. In 1931, the Wickersham Commission reported that prohibition was not being enforced because it was basically unenforceable. This led to the ratification of the 21 Amendment on December 5, 1933, which repealed the 18 Amendment.

The Mafia was reformed in 1930 under the leadership of Lucky Luciano. Believing that it was time to end the fighting and get back to the business of making money was Luciano's vision. Luciano began to modernize the Mafia by getting rid of the old bosses in the United States. On the night of September 10, 1931 Luciano's men, in the largest and best-orchestrated mass assassination in gang history got rid of 40 old-time bosses around the country (Haskins, 1974). New leaders followed these footsteps, the Mafia changed greatly in the 20thcentury. They began to operate legitimate businesses as well and the names of the leaders were kept secret.

Ethnic Gangs in Chicago

The Gang by Fredrick Thrasher, originally published in 1927, contained his study of the structure and activities of 1,313 gangs in Chicago. Thrasher was a member of the Chicago school of sociologists, His book is considered a classic in the field, and has greatly influenced subsequent studies. This work remains the prototype for other studies of delinquent gangs. One suitable conclusion is that gangs are just movable alliances made up of youth who are trying to work out their moving tribulations in gang activity (Thrasher, 1963). Thrasher noted that no two gangs were alike, but each was unique: "Wide divergences in the character of its personnel combined with differences of physical and social environment, of experience and tradition, give to every gang its own peculiar character. It may vary as to membership, type of leaders, mode of organization, interests and activities, and finally as to its status in the community. (p. 16)"

Thrasher (1963) described the transient character of membership in a gang. Many of the members participated in gang behavior for about three years, grew, married, and went on to young adulthood. Gangs having an official association were comparatively secure and would take on a name for themselves, such as the "Jets" or the "Dirty Dozen."

The formation of gangs such as the Dirty Dozen, "the natural outgrowth of a crowd of boys meeting on a street corner" (Thrasher,

1963, p. 40). As with many of the gangs in his study, Thrasher found that the basis of their configuration was spontaneous, fashioned by boys aged 16 to 22 who also spent their time loafing around at a street corner or pool hall. Thrasher also found that gangs had a home turf or territory. "The boys know every foot of ground, every nook and corner, of this region which they regard as exclusively their own and will defend valiantly against intruders" (p. 93). The Dirty Dozen, were attached to their local territory where they were used to hanging gout and occasionally, would stray off their turf into other territories. They were like other gangs in that they were ready to defend their territory against the encroachments of outsiders.

Gangs not only have a home territory, but also are aware of their enemy's territory. Like gangs of today, gangs of the past such as the Dirty Dozen had disagreements when they clashed with other neighborhoods, the public, and law enforcement. The Dirty Dozen were a tough gang and always fought together against other gangs. The attack of a rival gang only called for retaliation so the young gang members often carried and used dangerous weapons.

According to Thrasher (1963) found that gangs prevailed in the poverty belt of Chicago. In the inner-city region, gangs were found in the transitional (interstitial) area, which was characterized, by cultural separation, and which he describes in the following manner: "The gang is almost invariably characteristic of regions that are interstitial to the more settled, more settled, more stable, and better organized portions of the city. The central tripartite empire of the gang occupies what is often called "the poverty belt"—a region characterized by deteriorating neighborhoods, shifting populations, and the mobility and disorganization of the slum. It is to a considerable extent isolated from the wider culture of the larger community by the processes of competition and conflict which have resulted in the selection of its population, (p. 20)." He further found that among the mass of those who lived in the poverty belt, 82% of the boys, passed their leisure in the streets and were involved in gangs.

Though Thrasher (1963) is presenting one stage of life in the communities of Chicago, the development of gangs, the gangs and the type of life described in his work show what one may find among gangs today. There are other classics in the subject such as *Street Corner Society* (Whyte, 1943), *Street Gangs and Street Workers* (Klein, 1977), *Teen-Age Gangs* (Kramer & Karr, 1953), and *Gang Delinquency and Delinquent Subcultures* (1968). These are just a few that explain distinctiveness in gang societies. Materials of this caliber provide insight into the universal growth of gangs in the United States.

African American Gangs

The first major period of gangs in Los Angeles began in the late 1940's and ended in 1965 (Thrasher, 1963). There were African American gangs and Hispanic gangs in Los Angeles before this period, but they were small in numbers and little is known about the activity of these groups. Most of these gang members were family oriented and they referred to themselves as clubs but the police department often characterized them as gangs (Bond, 1936: p. 270). For example, some of the Black groups that existed in Los Angeles during the 1920's and the 1930's were better known as the Boozies, Goodlows, Blogettes, Kelleys, and the Driver Brothers (Alonzo, 1999). According to *Street Gangs* (2004) African American gangs have a 75-year history in Los Angeles, younger than its Latino counterparts. Gangs first appeared in Los Angeles in the 1920s, mainly in the downtown area where they first settled.

By 1920, the African American population in Los Angeles had increased more than seven-fold and new strategies for racial detention, such as restrictive accommodation covenants, emerged in tandem with the city's growth, according to Vigil (2002). The white community adopted this practice regarding a ruling a few years earlier, that made it illegal or unenforceable, and which remained in place for decades to come (Collins, 1980). Opportunities for

African Americans to live outside of the boundaries of the ghetto were still severely limited ten years later (Davis, 1992).

The fame of the Ku Klux Klan entailed its growth in the 1920s, which heightened discrimination promoted by the Los Angeles Playground Commission to politically prohibit and segregate African Americans from municipal swimming pools and (Vigil, 2002). For the next thirty years or so, Klan violence would happen again and again, but perhaps 1920s was the last decade in which such strong racist sentiments were so broad and blatant in Southern California (Vigil, 2002). However, "white Angelinos displayed a distaste for black neighbors, prompting black businessman H. A. Reeves to claim that ninety-five percent of the city's housing in the 1920s was restricted against blacks" (Tolbert, 1980).

Following to the depression, African Americans made their way to California, making it a most important goal. During that period, 1940 to 1950, the population of African Americans in Los Angeles grew by more than 100,000 (Gadwa, 1999). Sadly, African Americans suffered the highest unemployment rate of any group in the city (Lapp, 1987). Racial discrimination still existed and it continued to flare up in the early 1940s, forcing blacks to begin assembling in nearby areas, like down town Los Angeles, Watts, and the surrounding areas, (Gadwa, 1999). According to Vigil (2002), in 1941 white students threatened their African-American schoolmates burning them in image and displaying posters declaring, *"We Want No Niggers at This School."* Incidents of this nature were the primary means for African Americans to form street gangs as a defense against white violence within their (African American's) communities (Bond, 1936). The unemployment rate remained high for African Americans until war plants hired many African Americans because of the shortage of local labor created by the draft during WWII (Collins, 1980).

Once again after the war, discriminatory hiring practices by local industries and housing discrimination intensified. The population of African Americans was growing and so were the restrictive covenants to ensure that they (African Americans) remained confined by prewar boundaries, a containment that served only to worsen already congested living conditions (Bunch, 1990). Ironically, by the 1950s, the African American community in Los Angeles continued to deteriorate by remaining united within their own protection (Bunch, 1990).

Regardless of how racial barriers were relaxed and broken, the challenges that were created through the courts in the 1940s eased social restrictions but not economic obstruction (Vigil, 2002). Vigil further states that the African American community continued to get worse. An increased level of eccentricity and abandonment was forced on those African Americans living in the ghetto. In 1944, nearly one hundred frustrated Black youth who were denied jobs on the city's streetcar system attacked a passing streetcar and assaulted several white passengers (Collins, 1980: p. 29). From 1959 to 1965 unemployment rose from 12 % to 20 % overall, and to 30 % in Watts; and this did not include the fact that median incomes that declined by nearly a tenth (Vigil, 2002).

During the 1960s, conflicts among the Black clubs were growing, and as more white residents continued to move in and the white clubs began to fade, black clubs started turning the violence on each other. Even though 50 % of the gangs were Chicano/Latino, Black gangs represented a substantial ratio of gang incidents that were rapidly increasing in numbers (Study of Delinquent Gangs, 1962; 1). At this phase, black-on-black violence between the clubs was becoming a grave concern in Los Angeles.

By 1965, after the Watts Riots, the leadership of socially conscious organizations eradicated several of the clubs that had fought each other. Young black youth, became more politically aware and having greater concern for the social problems that beset their community. Alprentice "Bunchy" Carter, a former gang's member, was successful in transforming several Black youth gangs from South Central Los Angeles into radical activist against police brutality, (Hilliard & Cole, 1993 p. 218), and several organizations contributed to the cause. The Rebellion of 1965 was considered "the Last Great Rumble." As members of these groups buried their differences they came together in natural support against the reviled Los Angeles Police Department (Baker, 1988 p. 28, Davis, 1990: p. 297). A movement to build organizations and institutions which were led by and entirely responsible to the [Black] community was a result of the riot activity in Watts, (Bullock, 1999: p. 69).

Ethnic Gangs in Los Angeles

The historical study of the development of Chicano/Latino gangs in the City and County of Los Angeles reiterates the gang conditions of the past in other inner-city areas of the United States. *Homeboys* by Joan Moore (1978), relates the nature and development of the study of gangs by social scientists. She conducted her own study in East Los Angeles and San Fernando Valley where she interviewed gang members belonging to White Fence, El Hoyo Maravilla, and Los Polviados. In the early years of this century, Los Angeles became one of the most attractive areas to immigrants of many diverse nationalities. Immigrants who came to Los Angeles had few economic resources and they settled east of downtown in the present districts of Hollenbeck, Lincoln Heights, Brooklyn Heights, Boyle Heights, the North Main District, Belvedere, Maravilla, and City Terrace. These areas that are now dominated by a Chicano/Latino population. Dworkin (1983) are the same neighborhoods, from the late 1880s to the 1950s were populated by Irish, Armenian, Russian Molokan, Slav, Jew, and Mexican immigrants. "Each group turned the region into an area plagued by problems of crime, delinquency and tuberculosis" (p. 449). By 1926, a population of 90,000 people lived in the city and unincorporated portions of the county (Romo, 1983).

A repeating configuration driving the 20 century was the arrival of immigrants during the route of this century into East Los Angeles, which came under the consecutive influence of immigrants of all nationalities that set themselves up in an area. After acclimating to the city, they would move to other parts of the county. The province they left behind usually deteriorated as new immigrants of little capital moved in. Therefore, the poverty of the area has continued throughout the years. Since the Mexican colonization has remained comparatively steady throughout this period, the region east of downtown slowly became identified with the evermore prevalent, Mexican-American population. McWilliams (1949), noted that from the first years of the 20th century, the area was open to gangs of various nationalities, each working in and protecting their "turf" from enemy gangs of the or dissimilar ethnic descent. Slowly, after World War II, with the move of cultural populations to the region, the association of the gangs was mainly Mexican-American youth.

Chicano/Latino Gangs in Los Angeles

In contrast with the considerable amount of work that has been published on gangs and Chicano/Latino culture, studies of the history of Chicano/Latino gangs are few indeed. Moore (1978) notes that the study of Chicano/Latino gangs has been neglected; her study of three gangs in East Los Angeles uses the methods of the Chicago school of sociological community studies to study the relatively neglected Chicano/Latino gangs in this region. Moore traces the development of two Chicano/Latino gangs in her book *Homeboys*, in the East Los Angeles area, the two gangs are El Hoyo Maravilla, in the unincorporated Los Angeles district and White Fence in Boyle Heights. Reflecting the distinctive environment in which they grew up, these gangs were unique in their own way. For example, a reason for organizing the White Fence gang was that Chicanos/Latinos found themselves less prepared to defend themselves against other gangs within the area of East Los Angeles, so they bonded together. Moore further notes that the people living in Maravilla were considered only marginally adjusted to the life of the city. She found that schools in these areas placed little emphasis on academic subjects. Keep in mind that Spanish was the first language spoken in the home within the different barrios being represented. The lack of English fluency separated the Chicano/Latino from being accepted into other activities by non-Chicano/Latino youth and from levels of society within the city. As the population of the Chicano/Latino increased in East Los Angeles, including Lincoln Heights, Brooklyn Heights, and Boyle Heights, more gangs like White fence were formed in the 1940s. Her study of three gangs in the County of Los Angeles prompted Moore to hypothesized that the increasing use and distribution of drugs among gangs was a "rational" response to their inability to penetrate the labor market. In the hierarchy of the gangs, eventually the veteranos controlled the drug traffic that flourished among the gang members of the neighborhood. It is the belief of the researcher, that the breakdown of the family structure, the lack of education, housing, healthcare, and jobs are the reasons that gangs subsist in this modern era.

In his book *North from Mexico*, Carey McWilliams (1949), a lawyer and social critic describes the 1943 riots. Reveals a valuable resource in charting the historical evolution of Chicano/Latino gangs, their structure, and their activity. In his analysis of the events, he shows anti-Chicano/Latino bias to be found in the stories and editorials in the *Los Angeles Times*, *The Daily*, and *The Herald-Express*. McWilliams further notes the very active patterns of discrimination against the Chicano/Latino during the last century. Chicano/Latino adolescents, for the most part, attended inferior schools in the early years of World War II. McWilliams could not take part in youth activities with others his age in the various areas of the city. He could go to the municipal swimming pool only on Wednesday, only and the day the pools were drained and cleaned. This meant going to the skating rink as well. He and his friends were harassed if they appeared in groups in any other part of the city, including Hollywood. The Chicano/Latino adolescent, as stated by McWilliams states it, lived his life behind the "iron curtain" surrounding East Los Angeles.

McWilliams (1949) states that in August 1942, a young Chicano/Latino was found dead near the scene of a party in Sleepy

Lagoon, named thus by a young reporter because the body of Jose Diaz was found on a dirt road near an abandoned grave pit in East Los Angeles. The pit was used by Chicano/Latino youngsters as a swimming pool where a reporter named Sleepy Lagoon. Early in the day, a member of the 38th Street Gang had been assaulted by a rival gang. Suspecting a link between the two events, the police arrested 24 members of the 38th Street Gang, charging them with crimes ranging from assault to murder.

The name "Sleepy Lagoon" drew the public's attention to the 38 Street Gang's trial. Captain Ayers, Commander of the "Fourth Relations Bureau" of the Los Angeles Police Department, presented the evidence to the grand jury. While citing the poverty in which gang members grew up, he laced his testimony with extremely prejudicial opinions, accusing the Chicanos/Latinos as having an "utter disregard for human life" (Ayres, 1942, p. 142). The 38th Street Gang members were convicted in January 1943 of many charges stemming from the death of Jose Diaz in Sleepy Lagoon (Acuña, 1972). Later in the year, a District Court of Appeals reversed the decision citing the prejudicial content of the proceedings.

Soon after this, in June of 1943, extensive media attention focused on Chicano/Latino gangs. US Military servicemen cruised the streets of Los Angeles in a week-long rampage during which they beat up "pachucos", Chicano/Latino gang youth who were easily identified by their zoot suits.

1943 Race Riots and Pachuco Gangs

Servicemen stationed in Chavez Ravine during the race riots in June 1943 roamed the downtown area of Los Angeles cruising in convoys of taxis, as many (as 20 in a convoy), through East Los Angeles. Each time the servicemen found a Chicano/Latino youth, or a small group of pachucos, they proceeded to physically assault them. They also went into Chicano/Latino theaters in the downtown area and physically assaulted pachucos and other youth.

The police followed the servicemen at a distance, and arrested the pachucos after the servicemen left. A relatively small number of servicemen departed from the scene were arrested in these incidents. When military officials confined the servicemen to their bases, the riots would stop.

They published the time and place where the servicemen were to organize, the newspapers contributed to the racial fury. Therefore, thousands of civilians would join the servicemen to form mobs. Newspapers such as the *Daily News* that the "pachucos" (having learned a lesson), and that the beatings had a "cleansing effect. The *Los Angeles Times* spoke about dreadful situation created by gangs, such as their involvement in narcotics, strong-arm tactics, and other illegal activities. The gangs, as suggested by the editors of *The Times* were being organized by subversive political elements and could flourish due to "mollycoddling" treatment by police and politicians (McWilliams, 1983, p. 469). When the Mexican ambassador complained to the State Department, the Federal Government intervened and commanded that the U.S. servicemen refrain from engaging in violence against civilians or against pachucos, the local newspapers changed their tune.

Gang Structure and Activities from the 1940s to the Present

Finding a suitable definition of the term "gang" or "gang member" has been of difficult since no national standard definition exists. Originally, the word "gang" had a positive meaning. A gang was many people who formed a group and socialized together. Adolescents who gathered did so to break away from the family, to be independent, and to find their own uniqueness. Involvement in the group gave individuals a sense of belonging and significance.

Poston (1971) wrote: Street gangs have appeared in America since early in the nineteenth century, usually beginning as normal play groups, or as informal street corner clubs arising spontaneously out of friendships and mutual interests among small bands of youngsters who obtained thrills and satisfaction from being together. (p. 247)

The members of the group developed a shared uniqueness, which implicated the gang in activities ranging from gathering at street corners to committing unlawful acts such as theft, violence, and committing homicides. Law enforcement and probation officers describe the youth who joined gangs as follows: Most are extremely insecure underachievers with poor self-image, probably from a home where nobody's home, or where nobody provided much support, guidance or discipline. Their intelligence level corresponds to that of others their age. They're not dumb, and they're not monsters. They're people—some of them very likeable as personalities, some of them simply vicious, violent kids. (Burrell, 1980, p. 10).

In the current usage of the term gang, groups that are identified as gangs, generally come from the lower class of society. Gangs that have found their way into the suburbs originated in the city. This research incorporates studies of ethnic gangs in different cities of the country in historical presentation. What emerges is the fact that gangs, whether Irish, Italian, Chinese, or Jewish in New York City at the turn of the century, of African American gangs in South Central Los Angeles in the 1960s, or of Chicano/Latino membership in Los Angeles today possess familiar characteristics. Those characteristics are poverty, and inability to find employment and at times a language barrier. In addition, each gang has its own unique factors uniting the group in its gang activities.

Gang Characteristic

The period following WWII, to be the beginning of the era of the modern youth gang. Gangs are groups of minorities who live predominantly in urban centers of America. The post-World-War-II gangs are distinguished from those of preceding eras in the following ways:

1. the gang membership is younger

2. the nationality of the gang membership is primarily non-White, Black, Hispanic, Mexican—although Italians, Irish and other white ethnic groups still make up a significant percentage
3. drugs have become a greater and more publicized concern
4. gang activity tends to center around large-scale, well-organized street fighting resulting in death and injury to many of their members
5. fire arms and other lethal weapons are more readily available and more commonly used
6. their structure has become more rigid, with titled, designated leadership, and groupings by age or federations other groups
7. society has become concerned with the gangs as a social problem and attempts to understand them, to work with them and rehabilitate them, (p. 77).

Within the organizations, gangs are predominantly male, with females serving as auxiliaries to the gang. Typically, female gang members do not get involved in gang activities. Nevertheless, they can become very aggressive when they do get involved. Usually girls fight girls gang are important and serve many purposes for the male gang member. Their presence may help to "prevent or postpone delinquent episodes of a serious nature" (Kenney, Pursuit, Fuller, & Barry, 1982, p. 139). According to Short (1968), they truly are important as sex objects, hustles to be exploited, sources of prestige among the boys with whom they are associated, and. "Female auxiliary" groups are not uncommon. They exist they perform many functions for boys' gangs and enjoy a degree of autonomy among themselves (p. 4).

For the most part gangs vary in size, Gangs "usually remain small because of limitations of the size of their hang-out and problems with control and communication, but many are considerably larger than one may imagine" (Thrasher, 1963, p. 221). Thrasher reported gangs with memberships of up to 2,000. However, he relates that they usually start small and then may grow, with the original gang taking on the functions of an inner circle where the power lies. The additional cliques form from within the structure of the larger whole.

Gangs are territorial; they will identify with a neighborhood with clearly marked boundaries. The home territory is "gang turf" which has been claimed by that gang. West (1981) described gang territoriality as follows: "These street gang members perceive themselves as soldiers defending the honor of their neighborhood or barrio and will strike out at anybody they perceive as putting down their neighborhood" (p. 12). Territorial control provides security, stimulation, identity for the individual, and the gang seeks to maintain strict control to its boundaries.

The Youth Gang Task Force (California, 1981) pointed out the following reasons for joining the neighborhood gang:

1. Identity or Recognition—Being part of a gang allows the youth gang member to achieve a level or status he feels impossible outside the gang culture.

2. Protection—Many members join because they live in the gang area and are, therefore, subject to violence by rival gangs. Joining guarantees support in case of attack and retaliation for transgression.

3. Fellowship and Brotherhood—To most of youth gang members, the gang functions as an extension of the gang member's home environment. Many older brothers and relatives belong, or have belonged, to the gang.

4. Intimidation—Some members are forced into joining by their peer group. Intimidation techniques range from extorting lunch money to physical beatings. If a particularly violent gang war is in progress, the recruitment tactics used by the gang can be extremely violent, even to the point of murdering a non-member to coerce others into joining the gang (p. 12).

Characteristically, gangs tend to name themselves after streets in their neighborhood. They often tattoo the name of their neighborhood on their bodies, and this signifies an expression of territorial pride of the gang members. Carlos Marchena coordinator of the tattoo removal program at Homies Unidos in Los Angeles insists, "most of the youth tattoo the name of their neighborhood as part of recognition who they belong to," (personal communication, January 16, 2004). An additional characteristic for identifying and strengthening their territory is the appearance of graffiti on buildings and other structures in their neighborhood. The graffiti indicates which gang is in control of the neighborhood, and serves as a written language used extensively by gang members and is easily understood. Graffiti serves as a warning, to confront rival gangs; and often intrepidly announces the gang's victories, glories, and arrogance.

Youth Gang Structure

Youth gang makeup varies from a wanna-be group with an incessant change in membership to a formal organization with rules and regulations as Kramer and Karr (1953) noted: "The gang creature is a society of its own. It has its own laws, its own recognitions of merit, its own loyalties" (p. 211). The category and specific activity, or assignment, given to any one member of the gang depends upon his abilities, and affects how others relate to him. "Every person in the group performs his characteristic function with reference to others or, to put it another way, fills the individual niche that previous experience in the gang has determined for him" (Thrasher, 1993, p. 229).

The core divisions within a gang, whether the nucleus membership is small or large, include: the gang leader, an inner circle of leading members, and the core membership of actives. There are many inactive members who are considered retired within the organization, and, finally, the young aspirants who want to achieve the recognition, which will gain them entrance into the gang's main activities. Not all gang members are involved equally within the organization activities. For instance, the younger, less experienced youth who seek to become gang members run errands or engage in unlawful bustle to demonstrate their ability to withstand pressure. The core members of the gang "are typically the most violent, streetwise, and knowledgeable in legal matters" (California, 1981, p. 14). They are generally the ones who lead others in the gang's aggressive behavior; and have spent time in a State correctional institution for their aggressive behavior. According to Kenney et al., (1982), "core members are likely to be somewhat more aggressive and more deficient in personal skills and achievements" (p. 135).

"Gang leadership is best seen as 'functional' and distributed, i.e. leadership varies according to the activity in question and is a group function that can be and is assumed by numerous boys in different settings and as various times" (Kenney et al, 1982, p. 36). The leaders usually acquire their position through abilities, being bold in confronting danger, or being the "baddest guy around".

Members with precise talents that are useful to the gang are acknowledged, and they are appreciated for their talents. For instance, one member might be the "intellect" of the group, gaining a great amount of power because of his capability to think and plan. The "head" of the group may not become involved in the more aggressive, or violent organization activities. His thinking ability is needed by the organization, and this, in turn, gives him substantial power and freedom from participation in unsafe behavior.

In summation of, this chapter helps to identify the principal sources available for the historical analysis of Chicano/Latino gangs in the City and County of Los Angeles. The literature on ethnic gangs shows their expansion to gangs from their migrant beginnings as they gathered in their own ethnic communities within large cities. Many parallels among the ethnic gangs of the past and the modern Chicano/Latino gangs within the City and County of Los Angeles can be recognized: poverty, the barrio environment, unlawful behavior, use of firearms, and love media hype for their wrongdoings. These, and other parallels, will be presented in chapter six. The historical development of Chicano/Latino gangs in Los Angeles, presented in this chapter, illustrates that conflict and crime are intrinsic among Chicano/Latino gangs, with a long family tradition that most have learned to accept.

Chapter 3

Methodology

THE RESEARCHER COLLECTED ALL data beginning with the established literature on gangs. The researcher formulated questions that would be used in both prearranged and informal interviews. To assist the researcher, Luis Viscarra, a colleague from Homies Unidos, an organization that works with gang members and retired gang members, helped to develop a prearranged questionnaire. Once the questionnaire was constructed, the researcher approached agencies, organizations, and individuals for interviews knowledgeable individuals to acquire information on Chicano/Latino gangs in the City and County of Los Angeles. Each interview was conducted separately, and individually in depended from the other respondents.

During these interviews, the researcher asked questions verbally, and the responses were recorded on cassette tape with the permission of the respondents, or the researcher wrote them down. The respondents did not receive a copy of the questions before, during, or after the interviews.

On consideration of the atmosphere was comfortable for the subjects interviewed. They were not condemned nor judged them, and, in the process, honest responses were obtained. Six of the subjects were retired gang members, three were gang members, and the other five were not involved in gangs, but shared their information on gangs in Los Angeles. Six males and one female were interviewed each in his/her respective home, and the other three subjects were interviewed in the street outside their homes.

The average length of the interview was 90 minutes, and three interviews that lasted about two hours. Six interviews were recorded on cassette tape, three subject responses were written down on paper, and the other five, which were informed, were recorded by the researcher after the interview. Each of the respondents was given ample time needed to respond to the questions.

Information on gangs was gathered from the following agencies:

(a) The Gang Violence Bridging Project, an entity of the Edmund "G" Pat Brown Institute at California State University Los Angeles, where Gilbert Sanchez, Director of the Program, worked (the researcher worked under the supervision of Gilbert Sanchez, and spoke with Gilbert Sanchez during the period of employment with The Gang Violence Bridging Project);

(b) Retired California Youth Authority and Probation Officer, at Downey, where Don Irving was interviewed (Irving has worked in East Los Angeles for 35 years and has worked with many gang members, he offered information about gangs in the 1970s and 1980s);

(c) Adelante in Wilmington where Victor Bono was interviewed; one of my interviewees in Chapter 5;

(d) La Vida Sana in East Los Angeles where an interview was conducted with Mike Garcia, a Director, Consultant, and retired gang member known as "Cubano."

Two Intervention workers who shared their information on gangs were from Soledad Enrichment Action Inc (SEA) an organization that reaches out to the East Los Angeles and Boyle Heights community. The first Danny "Boxer" Garlar of Los Angeles provided the history of Chicano/Latino gangs when they first appeared in Ramona Gardens, in the 1950s to the best of recollection: The second, Johnny "Huero" Godinez, a retired gang member, grew up with gangs and went to school with gang members in East Los Angeles and Boyle Heights. Johnny spoke about his experiences growing up with gangs in the past and his experiences with the gangs now.

The other people interviewed were: Sofia, retired gang member from "Longos" in Long Beach; Tim Rodriguez, a veterano from Big Hazard; Alex Sanchez, a retired gang member from "La Mara Salvatrucha; Huero Waldo, a veterano from Big Hazard in Los Angeles a retired gang member; and Victor Bono, a veterano from "La Colonia" in the City of Watts.

Two sets of questions were designed by the researcher and were used in the interviews to collect information on gangs, gang history, and their development. Questions in "Set A" (see Appendix A) were used to interview non-gang members to gather general information from different agencies and organizations. "Set A" questions include a total of 32 questions and cover to four areas: 1) personal information, 2) gang-related data, 3) programs to control gangs, 4) and religious programs. Only those questions which applied to the subject being interviewed were asked. Questions in "(see Appendix B) were used in interviewing gang members and retired gang members. The questions were designed by the researcher to collect 67 items of information in four areas: personal; social, historical, and gang-related activities. "Set B" questions were administered to nine subjects; four were veteranos, (now retired gang members0, who could relate their experiences with gangs in the City and County of Los Angeles.

The type of questions in the four parts of "Set B" are as follows:

1. Part I was designed to collect background personal information from the subjects.
2. Part II was designed to collect information on the subject's personal involvement in gangs and the reasons for joining the neighborhood gang.

3. Part III A was designed to collect the historical data on all gangs, their activities, and their growth in number and membership.
4. Part III B was designed to collect information the historical beginning of the subject's gang.
5. Part IV was designed to collect information on the activities of the subject's gang, to determine whether the subject is still involved in the gang, and to find out the location of the gang if it is still active.

Limitations

This study was conducted by a single researcher and is based on research of the relevant literature and many interviews. Five gangs from the cities of East Los Angeles, and Boyle Heights were represented in the interviews, with the respondents ranging in age from 20 to 64 years. The interviews were limited to personal, family, and barrio life, and the history of gang related activity experienced by these individuals.

Nine interviews with three gang members and six retired gang members were conducted; however, only two are recorded in this thesis as case studies (Chapter 5). Information obtained from the other interviews was also utilized throughout this paper, but n to all the data gathered was transcribed due to its similarity of information.

Chapter 4

Mexican-American Heritage in the Southwest, Immigration Patterns, and Chicano/Latino Gangs in the City and County of Los Angeles

Mexican Settlement of the Southwest: 1840 to Present

A HISTORICAL BACKGROUND OF the social, political, and economic atmosphere in southwestern United States from the 1840s to the present is being presented to provide an understanding of the basic factors influencing the development of Chicano/Latino gangs in the City and County of Los Angeles. After review of the literature on gangs and Mexican-American history, this researcher recognized three major factors, which have prefigured the development Chicano/Latino gangs and contributed to their subsequent violence and unlawful behavior:

1. In the pattern of settlement of the Southwest Territories, Mexicans who became a majority of the population in the 1840s. They were displaced by English-speaking majority soon after the onset of the 1850s Gold Rush. This very rapid change, resulted in social, political, and economic discrimination against Mexican American. By establishing Chicano/Latino communities called barrios, the Mexican Americans responded to these changes.

2. The migration of Mexicans into the United States was influenced by the economics. Agricultural and industrial employers, were in demanded of cheap labor for development of the Southwest Territories.

3. Since the 1930s and 1940s Mexican American citizens have become increasingly active politically because of the Zoot Suiters, or pachuco movement, and due to the civil rights movement of the 1960s. The Chicano/Latino communities within the City and county of Los Angeles sought to act on discriminatory practices experienced. Some attempted to address the discrimination through legal means, while others use violent methods as. This chapter will describe these themes in more detail.

Chicano/Latinos Account for an Increasing Percentage in the U.S. Population

Latinos account for an increasing percentage of the U.S. population (Altarriba & Bauer, 1998). Their numbers have expanded due to the recent arrival of immigrant's large enough to account for 50% of this country's Chicano/Latino population (Smart & Smart, 1994). Stress due to acculturation, coexists with the rigors of immigration, and requires assistance from counselors as Chicano/Latino immigrants they adapt to their roles in a new society.

According to Ponce & Atkinson (1989), "Acculturation is a process whereby individuals learn about the rules for behavior characteristics of a certain group of people." Culture pertains to a people's way of life and includes the methods by which they extract a livelihood from their environment. Acculturative stress often has three aspects, which are of lifelong duration, pervasiveness, and intensity.

Acculturative stress is experienced in individual stages. Numerous theories of loss, transition, and adaptation assert the existence of stages of development that include initial relief, post-decisional regret stress with attendant psychological symptoms, and acceptance, adjustment, and reorganization (Smart & Snart, 1993). At first, an immigrant may feel relief after arriving on a new country and may wish for a better economic and political future. However, when confronted with an innumerable number of stressors, during this initial stage, the immigrant may come to question the decision to leave his or her homeland. Ultimately, if acculturative stress is conquered, reorganization takes place, wherein the immigrant adapts to losses and can re-adjustment his or her life.

Loss is described by Padilla, Cervantes, Maldonado, & Garcia (1998). Stressor events are conditions that are seen by the individual as inducing an important loss to the self or to the identity of the self. A pervasive feeling of anxiety and loss of control can be induced by lack of structure and lack of familiarity. Positive anticipation and feelings of control have been revealed to be a significant preventive measure against depression (Cervantes & Castro, 1985).

The will and ability to contend with life's challenges can be destroyed by the loss of identity and social support and attendant acculturative stress. The greater the level of acculturative stress, the less likely one is to invest in the progress of skills or the collection of resources that could be beneficial in perplexing circumstances. One is also less likely to use his or her abilities to prepare for or avoid problems. According to Smart & Smart (1993), the most stressful condition of the acculturation process is the re-evaluation of one's role within the new culture and a sense of not belonging. The more immigrants adhere to their ethnic identity, the greater the stress they experience and the lower their self-esteem becomes.

Cultural groups define and act on the acculturation process differently. Chicano/Latinos have unique immigration experience characteristics that are inclined to foster and support acculturative stress and obstruct movement through the stages of adjustment. To promote a healthy and complete adaptation response, counselors must become aware of differences between the European acculturation experience and that of Latino immigrants. As cognizance of these differences becomes more complete, counselors will become more skilled as cultural mediators and will be more able to amend acculturative stress.

The "melting pot theory" that has permeated much of American society, including legislation and social policy, originated from the migration experience of White Protestants from Northern and Western Europe (Ibrahim, 1991). These norms are no longer the reality, and American social policy must adjust to a changing ethnic and racial plurality. Counseling theory and technique, which plays a key role in many of the contacts between Hispanics and various educational, medical, vocational, and legal systems, must embody knowledge of the responsiveness to these unique Hispanic needs and to the acculturation issues they are likely to experience.

In U.S. culture, there is an inclination to discriminate against people based on color. According to Smart & Smart (1993), when a migrant comes from a country where he or she belongs to a racial majority, or where, as in Latin countries, racial mixtures are the norm, the experience of turning into a minority in the United States and encountering overt racial discrimination comes as a disorienting experience.

In many Latin countries, wide variation in skin color is the norm, and Hispanics are accustomed to accepting people of color. However, Americans of light-skinned Northern and Western European stock have tended to dichotomize people into the categories of "colored" or "white" (Altarriba & Bauer, 1998). With the label "colored" has come the tendency to distance and depreciate. Therefore, light-skinned Europeans have had a different acculturative experience because no matter what their country of origin they have not had to battle the instant discrimination that accompanies skin color. Light-skinned, young, and educated migrants usually experience a more favorable reception in the U.S. than do dark-skinned older, and uneducated newcomers.

In the U.S. discrimination against Latinos is still widespread. Ignorance, myth, suspicion, and misinformation continue. Regardless if the U.S. Constitution guarantees all citizens equal rights, Chicano/Latinos are still likely to experience unfair and prejudicial treatment in employment, education, housing, and other human services (Altarriba& Bauer, 1998).

In a culture that emphasizes cooperation, collectiveness, and strong intergenerational family ties, the pain of separation caused by migration is acute for Hispanics. Along with feeling lonely and isolated, the individual may also feel himself of herself to conflict with sociocultural expectations and consequently feel guilt and shame.

Loss of social support and family ties is distinctly acute for Chicano/Latinos, because Latinos cultures emphasize the sense of the collective over the individual by stressing affiliation and cooperation over competition and confrontation (Smart & Smart, 1994). A clash of cultural values therefore emerges when experiencing the American accentuation on separation and emancipation from family. It should not be a cause for wonder, then, that many immigrants feel vulnerable from the loss of social support after moving to the U.S. Loss of social support and kinship structure leads the immigrant to feel uncared about and undervalued. Self-esteem suffers, and the client is deprived of the sense of belonging to a social network and the sense of support that comes from implied mutual obligation. The gang members place and identity in the community and family is lost.

To the Chicano/Latino gang member and client, family is simply family, a place of retreat from the outside world (Marin, Otero-Sabogal, Marin, &Perez-Stable, 1985). In the Anglo-American family, the extended family older generation such as grandparents, and aunts and uncles are restrained from decision-making and there are few obligatory exchanges. In the Anglo-American culture, there is a clear distinction between an individual's family of procreation and the individual's family of origin. In contrast, in the Chicano/Latino American families, the entire extended family is a source of support and pride. There are significant reciprocal commitments between family members, and family relationships are intense and frequent.

Many Latinos, particularly Mexicans, enter the U.S. illegally. Immigration under these circumstances is distinctly stressful. Many Hispanics may have desires and plans of returning to their homeland when political and economic conditions permit (Ibrahim, 1991), therefore, they do not see their stay in the U.S. as permanent.

The Immigration Reform and Control Act of 1986 proclaimed an amnesty and entitled access to permanent citizenship (Ponce & Atkinson, 1989). Unfortunately, many did not take advantage of this opportunity and remain without legal status. Illegal immigrants do not have full access to jobs, education, and economic benefits and live in constant fear of deportation. If they are reported to the Immigration and Naturalization Services and are consequently returned to their country. Hence their lives are permeated by a sense of warnings and mistrustfulness.

Illegal immigrants are also susceptible to blackmail and corruption. They are often at the mercy of unethical employers who, when work is done, may report them to legal authorities as a means of escaping payment for work already completed. Illegal immigrants are also subject to working for below-market wages because of their legal status in the U.S. Although obtrusive exploitation is becoming infrequent, the threat of such coercion is ever-present and commits to a life-style of consistent instability and uncertainty.

Society and Professionals working as a team in the community must consider the distinct differences in acculturative experience between Latino immigrants and that of Europeans when dealing with acculturative stress. Social consideration can justify issues such as unique language needs, accurate assessment of the stress level, use of a "loss and adaptation" model, need for social support and social skill building, and familiarity with immigration laws (Smart & Smart, 1994).

Chicano/Latinos have displayed an astonishing language loyalty. The continued use of the Spanish language accounted for by the geographic proximity to Mexico and other Latin American countries. Because language is an essential part of the Chicano/Latino community, an initiative to provide services in the language chosen by the person must be taken. Where professionals are not fluent in Spanish, effective translators must be provided in the analysis of Chicano/Latino topics surrounding language and cultural sensitivity. Therefore, an analysis should be reviewed and include in an intervention process.

Because loss and adaptation are prevalent issues in the literature of Chicano/Latino acculturation, it may be relevant to integrate such approach into counseling interventions with Chicano/Latinos who are undergoing acculturative stress. In addition, because acculturation is commonly pervasive and long-lasting undertaking, it makes sense to put it in the framework of an adaptation or transition model of intervention, which also indicates and incremental stage process of noteworthy duration. There are a variety of such models which all have in common the idea of working through various stages of loss and adjustment until one ideally reaches a stage of adjustment, and successful coping.

Professionals who work with undocumented immigrants gang members, it is important to understand basic immigration laws and policies that lead to service delivery within the agency for which the counselor works. Insufficient knowledge of such matters leaves counselors opens to legal and ethical mistakes. One difficulty that may occur is the fact that in some circumstances, immigration law demands that undocumented immigrants be reported to Immigration Naturalization Service (Smart & Smart, 1994). This may cause a conflict of interest for professionals who must stabilize loyalty to the person against loyalty to the laws of the country. The fact that laws exit may make it complex for professionals to constitute trusting relationships with individuals who see professionals as portraying 'the system'. It becomes difficult to institute a productive and positive relationship without a certain degree of trust.

Because laws are disconcerting to immigrants and professionals their complexity promotes doubt and mistrust, professionals must invent tactics for working in such a manner as to deal with the acculturative stress that these circumstances impose. Two minimum prerequisites for sufficient services are access to direct and precise legal counsel, and clear explanation of public policy. Along with the understanding of immigration law and service guidelines, counselors must understand and enhance the acculturative stress that these regulations impose on Chicano/Latino immigrants.

The counselor's job must be done in congruence with and as a reflection of the society in which it is based. The arising reality of the American society is that of cultural diversity and quickly increasing numbers of gang members within our Chicanos/Latinos community. Reality for many Chicanos/Latinos involves the challenge of acculturative stress. American society will continue to change as different economic, political, and cultural forces interact in a consistent formation and reformation of the nation's life. By understanding the necessary losses and challenges that coexist with these changes, counselors can assist others in dealing with these changes and, in doing so, make positive contributions toward a fuller life for all.

A Brief History of Mexican Settlement of the Southwest and Los Angeles

Literature on Mexican American settlements in Southern California is to be found for the most part, in recent years, in volumes which contain contributions from many scholars on aspects of Mexican American culture (Acuña, 1972; Castro, 1974; Griswold del Castillo, 1979; Lamb, 1970; McWilliams, 1949; Moquin & Van

Doren, 1971; Romo, 1983; Samora & Simon, 1977). The majority population in the Southwest Territories was Mexican according to these researchers. The United States acquired a considerable section of the Mexican Territories, the Southwest, after the ratification of the Treaty of Guadalupe Hidalgo on February 2, 1848, and after the war with Mexico ended. This brought many changes to the Mexicans who resided in the territories. United States citizenship was offered to the Spanish-speaking people in the new acquired by territory, as a representation of one primary change. After assuming the unfamiliar territory, the United States government also assumed the constitutional responsibility for the Mexicans residing in the territories.

At the time, the Southwest became part of the United States, it was first a society of large Mexican ranches owned by Mexicans residing in the Southwest. The following factors operating in this Mexican society were of significance: 1) the people, both rich and poor, 2) shared a common language, and, 3) they identified with each other through cultural, religious, and belief of strong family ties. Jointly, all community members participated in the customary fiestas. As a result, the Mexican people of the Southwest United States established themselves as a well-stratified Mexican society, keep in mind that inequality still existed.

The Mexican people were given two choices as part of the Treaty of Guadalupe Hidalgo: (a) to move to Mexico within one year of the Treaty's effective date, or (b) to remaining in the United States and become American Citizens. Few people moved to Mexico because it meant destroying longstanding family and business ties and beginning anew. With longstanding family and business ties in the newly established United States territory already the majority remained. Those who remained "became a new element in U.S society—the Mexican Americans" (Samora & Simon, 1977, p. 100).

In the 1850s, the discovery of gold in California brought innovative ways that would completely transform the migration of Americans into the unfamiliar territory. The discovery of gold attracted people from all over the world, and all walks of life to the new lands in America, particularly to California. There had been very minor change throughout the previous century, and it was now time for meaningful change for the Mexican Americans.

Because of the transformation of society, it was not long before Mexican Americans realized that they had become outsiders in what they considered their homeland. Except than in the state of New Mexico, Anglo Americans soon controlled the government throughout the Southwest. Discrimination against Mexican Americans began once the Anglo Americans became the dominant majority.

All parts of the guarantees given the Mexican American by the Treaty of Guadalupe Hidalgo (1848) were violated. For instance, land was taken away from Mexican Americans because they could not legally prove rightful ownership. There were no official deeds. Due to this fact, the rich lost enormous land holdings and others suffered because they could not pay the taxes imposed upon them. They were forced to sell part or all their land to pay their debts. Because of their inability to speak English fluently, it was extremely difficult for them to take their grievances to the government and the courts. These wrongs were rarely corrected, even when their grievances went before the courts. Mexican American landholders lost lawsuits requesting property rights after their lands were illegally confiscated (Griswold del Castillo, 1979). The American government failed to provide equal rights to Spanish speaking Americans.

Mexican Americans were not accepted in the new American society, and they were an "uncivilized person, reduced to a state of inferiority by his language, his religion and his culture" (Samora & Simon, 1977, p. 100). The experience that Mexican Americans suffered caused them to detach themselves from Anglo society. Because of being forced to retreat into Spanish speaking communities to maintain their cultural identity; barriers were developed and continue to exist.

Barrios in Los Angeles

The purpose of this section is to provide a brief history about barrios or the Chicano/Latino communities, as they expanded from the original barrio in downtown Los Angeles Sonoratown. The origin of the barrio name: "Anglos and other European settlers who had to refer to the plaza section as 'Sonoratown' or 'Little Mexico'" (Romo, 1983, p. 5). Sonoratown received its name because of the many Sonorans who had immigrated to Los Angeles before 1850. Located north of First Street, Sonoratown was, initially a nostalgic reminder of Sonora, Mexico. A place of familial warmth and brotherhood, it changed as immigration into Los Angeles between 1850 and 1880 caused its expansion. As immigrants moved in, the old pueblo area became overcrowded, its buildings physically deteriorated, and the rich abandoned their townhouses. The Mexican Americans who has been residing in the area for a long time began to move to other areas of the county, leaving the barrio for the new immigrants who had no economic resources. "In 1850, Los Angeles, California, was the largest Mexican town in the United States" (Griswold del Castillo, 1979, p. xii).

Chicano/Latino families began to move to other areas in Los Angeles, particularly to East Los Angeles, by the 1870s. Griswold del Castillo (1979) describes the areas in which they began to establish their communities: "Only a few Mexican American families lived east of the Los Angeles river; these families Lived on Downey Street within the predominantly Anglo subdivision of American residences were more widely separated and integrated with their neighborhoods. Some families lived on small farms along Alameda, San Pedro, and Washington streets and others lived in small residences and shops located along Main Street" (p. 148).

New communities were established beyond the boundaries of the original neighborhood by the 1880s. The arrival of immigrants into Los Angeles caused an increase of Hispanics into other areas of the city. Those who moved had been long-term residents of the barrio, and they were craftsmen, merchants, engineers, and lawyers. They wanted to live in neighborhoods that were more affluent. They moved into the suburbs of Brooklyn Heights, Boyle Heights, and along Mission Street on the east side of the Los Angeles River (Griswold del Castillo, 1979). Sonoratown was then left for the poorer families and new immigrants.

There were two major reasons for the influx of immigrants into Los Angeles and the ensuing growth of the Hispanic population in outlying areas such as East Los Angeles. The first is that by 1910, industrial development and the infringement of commercial establishments in downtown Los Angeles pushed Mexican residents of Sonoratown into East Los Angeles. Secondly, there was a rapid increase in numbers of people fleeing the Mexican Revolution. They were lured into the United States by expectations of employment and a better life. During this period, the railroad companies were major employers of the Mexican immigrants in Los Angeles County. Railroads were needed to develop rail links between the downtown Los Angeles and the many new cities in the outlying parts of the Los Angeles County area. During this period from 1900 to 1920, Mexican railroad workers established their homes in East Los Angeles, San Pedro, Long Beach, Pasadena, Watts, and Santa Monica where the railroad labor camps were. Isolated urban barrios later evolved from these labor camps.

Barrios of East Los Angeles were preferred by Mexican Americans, and new immigrants because they could find food, shelter, work, and were familiar with the culture readily available to them. Between the years of 1930 and 1950, the population of Chicano/Latino neighborhoods increased greatly in the County of Los Angeles. Mexican immigrants no longer sought Sonoratown as their first home because there were many other barrios where family and friends were located. During this time Chicano/Latino in rural areas left to find work in the city. Even though, there was little employment in the city during the Great Depression of the 1930s, the situation changed by the World War II. Employers of the City of Los Angeles provided many opportunities for work for Chicano/Latino and other immigrants during the 1940s. Chicano/Latinos found semiskilled jobs in industries and women began to work in industry for better wages than agricultural workers.

For those who preferred agriculture work, farming increased in the rural areas of the county. San Fernando Valley farms provided job opportunities in the agricultural fields and in the packinghouses. Because of additional job opportunities, Chicano/Latinos families in the San Fernando Valley barrios of Pacoima, Canoga Park, Van Nuys, and others grew in population. Encountering problems of discrimination, Chicano/Latinos continued to settle within the City and County of Los Angeles establishing more barrios.

The residents enjoyed recognition with each other through clothing, language, behavior, food, culture, and religion within the barrio community. Being a part of the community, they lived in, provided them with a sense of pride, security, and an awareness of their cultural heritage. In his book *The Los Angeles Barrio*, 1850-1890, Griswold del Castillo (1979) writes: "With the Anglo conquest, the term 'barrio' took on a special meaning, signifying the region of the town where only the Spanish speaking lived" (p. 140). The barrio provided Chicano/Latino with inexpensive housing, and work opportunities for Spanish speaking people. Coming into Los Angeles, new immigrants learned how to survive in the city by shared experiences of those already established in the neighborhood. Until they could find a better place, immigrants found companionship and a place to live within the barrio, (see, Sanchez, 1993).

In short, Mexican Americans were shifted from their accustomed locations with the changes that came about after the capture of the Southwest Territory by the United States. Bucolic society was transformed into urban society and, Spanish-speaking people could hold on to their culture through the materialization of the barrio, which is the birthplace of the present-day Chicano/Latino gangs.

Immigration Patterns Related to Economics and Political Factors

Chicano/Latino that settled within the City and County of Los Angeles were attracted, and influenced strongly by the economic attractions of the area. In addition, the economic advantages provided by work opportunities in the Southwest encouraged migration by Mexicans into the United States. These opportunities were later countered by the political moves to halt immigration, by repatriation policies of the 1930s. Years of turmoil followed for many Chicano/Latino families, whose members were split apart, and forced to live on both sides of the United States Mexican border. The demand for cheap labor brought about by the World War II, again provided a momentum for Mexican immigration into the United States as the "Bracero" program was instituted. This segment will expand the political and economic atmosphere in the United States in this century to exhibit the factors influencing the significant increase in the Chicano/Latino population in Los Angeles.

Immigration from Mexico into the United States before 1900 was confined solely to the border states of Arizona, California, New Mexico, and Texas. Movement back and forth across the border was easy, since these states were formerly Mexican territory. Some relatives would come to visit their families, while others arrived in the United States to work and live. There were periods of mass migration of Mexicans into the United States, especially during the gold rush, when large numbers of Mexicans joined in the search for gold. Griswold del Castillo (1979) described the scale of this migration: "The ferryman at the Yuma crossing, Dr. Lincoln, reckoned that between 1848 and 1852 almost 25,000 Mexican immigrants from Sonora crossed into California on their way to the gold fields" (p. 38).

Another reason for Mexican migration from the 1800s to this very day has been the magnetism of employment and good wages. A clear majority of those who emigrated from Mexico came to work in the United States would send money home to their families. As they discovered a higher standard of living in the United States, many chose to stay. Moquin and Van Doren (1971) noted that: "During the period from 1880 to 1900 the Mexican-born population of these border states increased from 66, 312 to 99,696, a gain of 33,657 in twenty years" (p. 334).

A third major factor influencing the immigration of Mexicans into the United States was the industrialization of the Eastern states. The promises of good wages drew thousands of Americans into the cities, thus leaving behind their small farms in rural areas. There was general concern that not enough crops would grow to feed the increasing population in the cities. The government believed the virgin lands in the West had the potential to be formed to feed the nation. The two key issues, in developing an agricultural empire in the West were: (a) how to get the agricultural products from the West to Eastern cities, and (b) the labor requirements for agricultural work. The Mexican worker filled both these voids. Chicano/Latino families were important for providing the required farm labor and were also cheap labor for the railroad companies who were building the cross-country railroads. The Chicano/Latino population of the border states increased as industrialization opened more fields of employment for unskilled laborers in the mines, railroads, factories, and agriculture.

The Mexican Revolution was a significant factor affecting immigration from 1910 to 1920. A considerable and enduring movement of Mexicans into the United States occurred after the defeat of President Porfirio Diaz's government in 1911. One president after another was either overthrown or murdered, bringing what possessions they could carry. Thousands of immigrant families of various social levels came to the safety of the border lands in the southwestern United States. "Immigration statistics record an increase from nearly 22,000 persons in the 1905-1909 period to almost 83,000 in 1910-1914 and 91,000 in 1905-1919" (Grebler, 1966, p. 20).

There were additional political events that drew Mexican immigrants into the United States in the early years of this century. Demands for farm and factory products increased during World War I. Mexican immigrants filled the labor shortage in the Southwest, and those who came north were attracted to urban centers such as San Antonio and Los Angeles. Many individuals arrived in Texas and then migrated to California.

During the 1920s the Chicano/Latino population increased in the City of Los Angeles, and big farms and ranches were located throughout the County of Los Angeles. With the improvement of technology, factories and canneries were built, Chicano/Latino workers then began to move to the cities, a trend which was occurring throughout the Southwest, and Los Angeles becoming a unique city. According to Samora and Simon (1977), "by 1935, Los Angeles had the largest community of Mexicans in the world outside of Mexico City" (p. 120).

Approximately 925,000 Mexican Nationals crossed into the United States from 1910 to 1930. Twice as many people immigrated into the United States during the 1920s as the number of Mexicans who left Mexico during the Mexican Revolution. In the decade of the 1920s immigration from Mexico peaked "with some 500,000 reported as entering on a permanent visa" (Gerber, 1966, p. 21).

Repatriation Policy

Immigration from Mexico proceeded unimpeded until the Great Depression of the 1930s. Strongly affecting the Chicano/Latinos residing in the United States, the Depression was catastrophic to most of the population in the United States. One main reason for this stems from the fact that agriculture in the United States was in crisis, and the demand for farm work decreased sharply. Public officials voted to send them back to Mexico rather than to provide them with public assistance/welfare. A federal policy of repatriation of people of Mexican descent began, as Grebler (1966) stated: "The repatriation took so many forms that the whole issue is clouded in semantics. The return movement to Mexico in the 1930s included a huge twilight zone between voluntary and forced migration, and "repatriation" is used here as a generic term for all kinds of departures (p. 25)." Chicano/Latinos were" rounded-up" and sent back to Mexico, while others left of their own choice. Repeatedly, families were broken up when the father, mother, or both being aliens, were repatriated, while their children, as American born citizens were sent back to Mexico with their parents despite their legal status as citizens. According to Grebler (1966): Nearly 89,000 Mexican aliens departed in the 1930s while 27,000 immigrated on permanent visa. Deportations and other expulsions under federal proceedings, which are not included in the above figure on out migration, were also at an elevated level. The magnitude of the Exodus is illustrated (through not measured) by the decline in the Mexican born population in the United States from 639,000 persons in 1930 to little over 377,000 in 1940 (p. 29).

World War II and the Bracero Program

Immigration policies which had restricted the entrance of Mexican National into the United States were reevaluated, because the United States had just entered World War II in December 1941. A labor shortage came into existence because of our young men getting engrossed into the armed forces. Officials from the United States negotiated with the Mexican government to establish a temporary labor program, known as the Bracero program. This program provided wartime labor for American agriculture by employing braceros, the term applied to the Mexican citizens who were allowed entry for purposes of work. Even though, this program was meant to be temporary, it was not terminated until December 1964. Throughout World War II, employment opportunities existed in the cities as well as the bucolic areas, and Mexican Americans migrated to urban centers in the 1940s. Numerous Chicano/Latino from the Southwest migrated into California as those who came up from Mexico migrated into Texas, New Mexico, Arizona, and into California as well.

Illegal immigration by Mexican Nationals across the border was encouraged by economic attractions of work and good wages. In the initial stages of the bracero program, there were also illegal aliens working side by side with legal entrants into the United States.

This encouraged American employers to hire illegal entry workers because they accepted lower wages.

Responding to the large arrival of illegally entering Mexican Nationals, the United States government initiated "Operation Wetback" in the 1950s. The program was put into effect at the border states, then extended to the interior states. A massive round up and repatriation of illegal aliens was begun in June 1954. Samora and Simon (1977) described this situation as follows: Over one million Mexican illegal aliens were apprehended in 1954 alone. The number of subsequent years declined but began to increase again about the middle of the 1960s and, now, is increasing at a very rapid rate. (p. 145)

The Chicano/Latino population in the United States had increased, despite the expulsion of illegal aliens. Mexican immigration on permanent visa since the 1940s and 1950s has added to the Chicano/Latino population in the Southwest. According to Grebler (1966): "Immigration on permanent visa began to accelerate in the early fifties. Entries of this type increased steadily from 6,372 in 1951 to over 64,000 in 1956, a number exceeded only in 1924 and 1927 and not surpassed in any subsequent year. In the decade, nearly 293,500 were recorded, and the share of Mexicans in total immigration exceeded 15 percent in the second half of the 1950s" (p. 33). In the early 1960s, permanent immigration from Mexico was at an elevated level, but was followed by a sharp decline when administrative controls became effective July 1, 1963. "In the first half of the decade nearly 218,000 Mexicans came on permanent visa, a rate exceeded only in the 1920s" (Grebler, 1966, p. 36). To further describe the situation Grebler writes: "An abrupt change occurred in 1964; less than 33,000 Mexicans were admitted as against over 55,000 the year before" (p. 36). Since 1964, then, restrictions and tighter controls by the United States have made it very difficult for immigrants from Mexico to obtain a permanent visa; nevertheless, illegal aliens still cross the border looking for economic opportunities.

Because of increased movement of Chicano/Latino families from rural areas to the cities, by the late 1960s, about 80% of the Chicano/Latino population was in urban areas. During these factors, which have encouraged the entrance of Mexican National into the United States, Chicano/Latinos now constitute the largest ethnic minority group in the southwestern United States, with California leading the nation. Los Angeles has the largest Chicano/Latino population of any city in the United States (U.S., Department of Commerce, 1982).

Factors Influencing the Increase of Political Activity by Chicanos/Latinos in Los Angeles County

Based on the previous historical developments, it is clear that the County of Los Angeles had a large Chicano/Latino population by the 1930s, which has increased to the present day. Since Chicano/Latinos have participated more in the United States work force, as they attended schools in the United States, and as they learned to speak English, they wanted to partake more fully in the social, political, and economic benefits in the United States. Nevertheless, the Chicano/Latinos acutely felt the discrimination against them in all three areas of participation. They responded to discriminatory practices in many ways, as illustrated by the following:

1. The mode of dress and the violence of the pachuco gangs of the 1930s were in protest to Anglo society and the economy of the times.
2. There was a demand for increased social, political, and economic benefits by World War II veterans of Chicano/Latino origin who wanted to enjoy the full benefits of their United States citizenship. Their activities were the precursor for the Chicano/Latinos and the Civil Rights movements of the 1960s.

3. There was increase in the number and violence of youth gangs as freeways and other factors served to increase the numbers of barrios in the county.

This segment reviews these responses in more detail to understand the strength, determination, increased number, and violence of Chicano/Latino gangs in the County of Los Angeles.

Early Chicano/Latino Gangs

Concentrated in large settlements, set apart from other youth because of the color of their skin and their language, Chicano/Latino youth experienced discrimination and unrest. Chicano/Latinos were rebuffed in schools for speaking Spanish and discriminated against in employment and housing, which made them feel as if they did not belong in this Anglo society. Being identified by Anglos as "Mexican," and not "American," led Chicano/Latinos to identify strongly with the barrio and its people because of the attitude of non-acceptance. According to McWilliams (1946), "by 1904 there were 36,000 'Mexican' youngsters in Los Angeles between the ages of 6 and 17, 98% of whom were American-born" (p. 318).

These youths created social gangs, which increased as new Chicano/Latino youth immigrated into the area and joined the barrio gang, and frequently, fought among themselves because of their differences in background. For example, there was conflict between youth of Los Angeles and those who came from Texas. There has always been conflict between the resident Mexican Americans in Los Angeles and newly arriving immigrants. No formal record of gangs and their numbers exists, so it is difficult to assess the number of gangs in the County of Los Angeles between 1850 and the 1920s. the only information available is the testimony of gang members themselves who are familiar with the history of their gang. An article in the Herald Examiner stated: Local Hispanic gangs trace their roots to the 1890s and the influx of Mexican immigrants. The new residents lived in neighborhoods with people from native Mexico. Rivalries between neighborhoods developed into open combat, and gangs were formed immigrants, as well as existing gangs that patrolled already established neighborhoods. (Furillo, 1983, sec. A, p. 8). About involvement in gangs in the forties, "Huero" Waldo states: "Back then joining a gang was the thing to do because there wasn't anything offered to us. There were no jobs, and school didn't teach anything because we spoke mostly Spanish, and nothing was offered in the barrio."

Gang members already in their late 20s and early 30s had been involved in gang life for many years. The youngsters including myself, we aspired to become a gang member because we saw others joining gangs, and in gangs who were the older leaders (Personal communication, October 12, 2003). Another retired gang member; Mike 'Cubano' Garcia described the gangs in the late forties and fifties as follows: "I was involved in gangs in the County of Los Angeles at the age of eight years old, when I first went to Juvenile Hall, I got involved with gangs because I wanted to be identified and I wanted people to know where I was from, and what I stood for. I survived because I held my own inside and allowed no one to run over me." I started out by stealing trivial things to gain recognition from the older homies who were involved in the neighborhood. I also made sure that I dressed like the older homies who wore zoot suits, because, that was the trend back then.

Most of the homies were between the ages of 15 and 20 years old, and some were even younger. Quite a few youngsters were put in juvenile hall because of their mischievous behavior, but the cops always put the blame on the gang. (M. Garcia, personal communication, September 16, 2003). Chicano/Latino gangs were prominent in the San Fernando Valley by the late 1930s. Moore (1978) mentioned gangs such as the "Chain Gang," "Los Raceros," "Los Polviados," (The Powder Puffs). The "Polviados" from San Fernando "would cruise 'enemy' territories, fighting with knives, tire irons, chains, bottles, and baseball bats" (p. 71).

According to "Huero" Waldo (2003), the use of dangerous weapons by gangs in East Los Angeles began in the 1930s as means of protection, and their use escalated from then on. "In the 1940s, gangs had knives, guns, and submachine guns, because weapons gave them more power over other gangs and they were feared greatly" (personal communication, October12, 2003). Much of the fighting between gangs occurred when a gang went into another neighborhood to do damage, and that was when the barrio gangs began to use more violence to protect the neighborhood from intruders, anyone not from that neighborhood was considered an enemy or outsider.

Now, small gangs surfaced in other areas: Long Beach, Wilmington, and the San Fernando Valley. As gangs proliferated, gangs from different cities became rivals.

Pachuco Gangs

Among Chicano/Latino youth in the 1930s, a culture known as pachucos began in Los Angeles, and this group could be identified by their language and behavior as well as their clothing. The pachuco introduced a new form of dress, talk, and manner of walking and standing. These traits distinguished him from all other gangs. His style of dress was the "zoot suit" and a black or brown hat. The pachuco dialect was a mixture of Spanish and English introduced into Los Angeles by Mexican Americans from Texas (Garcia, persona communication, September 16, 2003). The dialect was spoken by youths whether they were members of gangs or not, and it is used to this day by barrio gangs, the "Low Rider" (a Chicano/Latino car club organization), prison gangs, and others. Chicano/Latino gangs used very violent means by the 1930s, to bring attention to their activities. The general frustration of Chicano/Latino youth over their inability to overcome discriminatory practices led to the pachuco culture and eventually the Zoot Suit Riots.

Pachucos forming gang's known as zoot suiters attracted national attention during the riots of 1943 in Los Angeles. Moore (1978) describes the symbolism of the pachuco dress and dialect in their protest Anglo society: The zoot suits worn by the Chicano/Latino gang boys of 1942 and 1943 had huge oversized trousers and accessories that gave the new wartime austerity regulations (narrowly cut trousers and no cuffs) the finger, a gesture of symbolic challenge. Such a challenge, of course, immediately attracted attention at dance halls (p. 37).

In June 1943, during the Zoot Suit Riots, servicemen came into Los Angeles beating up zoot suiters and stripping them of their clothing. The Police did little or nothing to prevent this practice, and then would take the zoot suiters to jail, blaming the riots on them. The pachucos continued into the 1950s, and Danny "Boxer" Galar described Chicano/Latino gangs as follows: In the 1950s there were many pachucos in the Los Angeles area, and you see them everywhere with their zoot suits, chains, double-soled shoes, and their ducktail haircuts. These gangs were always getting into trouble and causing fights (Personal communication, June 30, 2003).

Mike "Cubano" Garcia said this about gangs in the 1950s:

> Chicano/Latino gangs were in every community within the County of Los Angeles. When I was locked up in County Jail during the 1950s there were gang members from every neighborhood in the county that were locked up at the same time. They had gotten involved in gangs for protection from other gangs, which were rivals to their neighborhood. They would gangbang (fight), smoke marijuana, and take drugs, such as heroin, reds, yellowjackets, and quaaludes. Drugs were hard, but we didn't have all this synthetic stuff like we have today, such as rock cocaine, ice and so on.
>
> Most of the youngsters who got involved with gangs were over 14 years old. You didn't have 9 and 10-year-old kids getting involved with gangs, using drugs, and selling their bodies like today (Personal communication, September 16, 2003).

The Effect of World War II

The Second World War served as the most important single event in changing the lifestyle of the Mexican American population because many Mexican Americans were drafted or volunteered to serve in the American Armed Forces where they learned new trades. Those who returned from the war became dissatisfied with their previous condition of subordination, low-paying jobs, and discrimination. This is when the Chicano/Latino recognized the need for unity within his own sector, and with an increase in the Chicano/Latino population came a need to fight for first-class citizenship as Americans. The Civil Rights Movement of the 1960s within the Chicano/Latino communities was an effort to bring change to discriminatory practices against them and their people. The meaning of the barrio or neighborhood was that it allowed the Chicano/Latino to maintain a sense of identity with their culture. Consequently, Mexican Americans educated their sons and daughters, some becoming lawyers working in defense of Chicano/Latinos on trial. Some groups formed formal organizations to promote ethnic consciousness and pride among the Spanish-speaking community members. These ethnic pride groups sponsored social and political activities, for instance, "La Raza" (literally, the race) was formed, a concept of "our cause" which was an attempt by Chicano/Latinos to move forward politically and economically.

Communicating their experiences, news, and political events, a Spanish-language press developed and gave the local newspaper an opportunity to point out the wrongs and the victimization which took place against the members of the Chicano/Latino community by the Anglo majority. Through the press, the people voiced their grievances against discrimination, unequal services, segregation, and unequal rights. Griswold del Castillo (1979) states in his book *The Los Angeles Barrio* that the Mexican American press was important in developing and maintaining community awareness as early as the 1880s: Besides developing ethnic awareness by pointing out group victimization, the Mexican American press also developed a sense of community in more positive ways. This was especially true in their reporting of Mexican Independence Day celebrations, lasting from September 15th through September 27th (later changed to the 15th and 16th, and the Cinco de Mayo celebration of the defeat of the French forces in Mexico in 1862. They advertised accounts of festivities (p. 131)."

The Increase in Numbers of Gangs and Gang Violence

A factor contributing to the rise of gangs in the County of Los Angeles in the 1960s and 1970s was the construction of freeways. Neighborhoods were divided as freeways were constructed: one neighborhood frequently was broken up into two or three different barrios, on opposite sides of the freeway. Gangs would take on the name "Westside" or "Eastside" depending on which side of the freeway they were located. As a result, freeways became scars across the County of Los Angeles, separating similar Chicano/Latinos communities from each other. That's when new gangs formed in the newly created freeway land pockets.

Paradoxically, in another sense, the freeways provided easy access to other parts of the county. Neighborhood or barrio residents could maintain communication with their friends and families who left the neighborhood for other parts of the county, because the freeways allowed fast travel from one community to another. In the sixties and seventies, due to urban renewal and the desire among Chicano/Latino parents to raise their families in a better environment, many Chicano/Latino families moved to the remote suburbs of the County of Los Angeles. In doing so, parents unwittingly contributed to the spread of gangs. Since their children had already lived in a gang environment, they formed gangs in the new neighborhoods. These new gangs claimed the unfamiliar territory as their own. According to Junior Payon (name changed in this thesis), in the 1960s and 1970s youths wanting to start a new gang could begin in the manner he did: Twenty years ago, my homie and I started our own clique in the neighborhood. We didn't want to be part of the other cliques, which was already in there. We really didn't want to go through their initiation process. I was only 15 years old, and had earned my respect and didn't have to prove anything to anybody. I had my battle scars and the neighborhood respected me. My homies approved of the new clique and we started recruiting," (Personal communication, March 22, 2003).

Irving (2001) comments on the expansion of gangs in the County of Los Angeles: Chicano/Latino gangs in East Los Angeles go back from sixty to eighty years, while the more recent gangs outside of Los Angeles go back about 20 years. The expansion of gangs, I think, is all predicated on how the original city started and expanded. The heart of the nucleus is going to be where the original city was, Los Angeles to Chicano/Latinos. East Los Angeles is basically downtown Los Angeles to Chicano/Latinos. So, the people who settled in East Los Angeles years and years ago is where the seeds were planted, and as people moved out of the area from central Los Angeles, other gangs began to form.

Today in the community you've got many gangs. East Los Angeles gang territory is extremely well defined—it can be divided by one street, one gang on one side, the other gang on the other side of street. A lot of the gangs are compacted together—they are just jammed right up into the ghetto every third or fourth block, or on every eighth block there is another gang. Gangs have expanded as people moved out from Los Angeles. About 10 years ago communities had gang problems out in the San Gabriel Valley toward Pomona, West Covina, and Azusa. As people migrated away from Los Angeles into the suburban neighborhoods, little pockets of gangs and new gangs began to pop up in the new communities. People migrated in hope of getting away from the high gang, high crime and the bad type of influence for their children, They, in fact, brought some of those bad children/youth with them, perhaps not recognizing that their children could have been just as big a problem as anyone else's children. So, you had gangs flourishing all over as guys from East Los Angeles started a Clique of their own and built a gang in the suburban communities (Personal statement, July 23, 2001).

Gilbert Sanchez characterizes the Chicano/Latino gangs as follows: The street gangs with which we are dealing today are third and fourth generation gangs. There are more Chicano/Latino youth joining these gangs who have had their parents, cousins, and friends involved in gangs, many of these youths are very young—9—10—11—12—13 years old who just can't wait to be 16 years old to really get into the action and be somebody among his friends, be just like them when they get older" (Personal communication, April 19, 2002).

Chicano/Latinos joining gangs in the County of Los Angeles from 1970 and 1980 have been as young as eight years old, and parents of these children seem unable to do anything about it. Youth that are encouraged to join gangs join, because of an older family member or relative that already is an active gang member. The young boys and girls begin their socialization process into the gang early by dressing and speaking as the "homeboys" and "homegirls" of the barrios do. One should keep in mind that many time these children become victims because the parents promote this life style in the home. Garcia describes the strong attraction of the gang for Chicano/Latino youth:

> As many gangs as there are today, many youths will be joining them because they are going to want to be machos or vatos in their neighborhood as others have been before them. Gangs in the barrios have been around for many years and have been passed on to the younger generations. Just the other day there were these little boys about eight or nine years old asking another nine-year-old boy who just moved into the neighborhood not to join the gang which was across street but to join their gang. These little boys don't know it, but they are heading into more serious things and problems because they are already cliquing (M. Garcia, personal communication, September 16, 2003).

In 1979, in the County of Los Angeles, it was est4imated that there were 300 different gangs with a total of 30,000 members per gang. Of the 61 cities of the County of Los Angeles with populations of 20,000 or more, 42 had gangs within their communities, and about 80% of those gangs were identified as Chicano/Latino gang members. Sherman Block, Sheriff of the County of Los Angeles, estimated that there were about 400 gangs with 30,000 members in the county, and further stated that the membership is growing.

It was in the 1970s that Los Angeles became aware of the full extent of the gang problem and the need to find solutions to it. Though gangs continued to be a pressing problem in Los Angeles in the 1980s, inroads have been made by community organizations so that Chicano/Latino youths are now being "educated" to grow up without joining violent gangs.

Chapter 5

Case Studies in the Form of Oral Interviews

TWO ORAL INTERVIEWS WITH retired gang members of two Chicano/Latino gangs in Los Angeles are recorded in this research. These interviews are included as a means of determining why the reasons Chicano/Latino youth join gangs, why they participate in violent gang activities, and why they remain in the gangs for years. These two interviews with Victor Bono and Huero Waldo were selected from nine interviews for inclusion here because they provide clear insights into the motivations of Chicano/Latino youth who join gangs.

Bono, born in 1940 but was involved in gangs since 1956, now age 64, has knowledge of gangs in Los Angeles, which goes back into the 1040s even before he became a gang member. His testimony represents a great overview of gangs in the area, and the experience of Huero Waldo then represents a view of gangs in history, past, present, and future. To add to the importance of the study of these two gentlemen is the fact that they reformed their lives, demonstrating a concrete basis for hope of reforming gang members.

The other seven respondents in oral interviews provided information about Chicano/Latino gangs, which been used throughout this research. Their entire testimony was not presented here because much of the respondents' answers reiterated the comments of the persons whose responses are recorded in the chapter.

Before conducting the interviews, the respondents were informed by this researcher about the project, and they both agreed to allow the audiotaping of the interviews. The text presented here is a transcript of these audio-tapes of the interviews. Where the interviewer's comments have been included, they have been placed within brackets this transcript. The researcher's questions were not submitted to the respondents prior to the interview. This researcher asked the questions for the first time during the interview.

Oral Interview #1

The interviewee was Victor Bono, a retired gang member and veteran of the "Quarter Gang" a gang in Watts, a city within the County of Los Angeles. Now an intervention worker Bono spends his time doing outreach work in hopes that he can reach these youth of today. Bono was involved in gangs from 1956 up to 1967 when he was sent to prison. Now 64, he has resided in the County of Los Angeles all his life. His involvement with gangs began at the age of 16, but he remembers gang activities that went back as far as the forties. For 11 years, he was involved in gang activities and the drug trade in Los Angeles. Bono spent the next 31 years in a Federal prison where he kept his gang mentality. He was released in 1998 and he now spends his time doing outreach work among other things.

Interviewer: Are you/were you a gang member?

Bono: I used to be involved with gangs in Los Angeles for many years. I started getting involved at the age of 16 in 1956. All my life I have been in and out of jail and prison, including juvenile hall. When the zoot suiters were around, I had an admiration for them because my whole family came from that era. The zoot suiters were known as pachucos, and now they are known as homies in the neighborhood. Keep in mind that the transition of the pachucos faded out. Even though I broke away from gangs in a negative way, I still am very much involved in the lives of these youngsters of today.

Interviewer: What's the name of the gang you associated with?

Bono: When I first got involved with a gang, the name of the gang was the Quarter Gang and the name of the neighborhood was "La Colonia" in the City of Watts back in 1956.

Interviewer: When did you first notice gangs in your neighborhood?

Bono: Gangs in Los Angeles have always been in existence. As a young kid growing up around "Maravilla" a neighborhood in East Los Angeles. I used to see the older homies already partaking in the gang life. The older vatos were the one that carried the tradition and introduced the younger homies to the neighborhood. Some of the vatos were 18 to 20 years of age, and some were older. In the old days, the children born in the neighborhood became a "soldier" when the elders taught them the rules of the game. As they grew older, the youngsters fell into a different t category and got into something else.

Interviewer: When did you begin your association with gangs?

Bono: At the age of sixteen, in 1956, I started off by doing things like stealing to be recognized by the gang.

Interviewer: How old were you when you became a gang member?

Bono: I was sixteen years old. In them days you did not have young kids getting involved into gangs.

Interviewer: How did you become a gang member?

Bono: In the 1950s and through the 1960s there was no initiation process as there is today. In those days, people who lived in the neighborhood joined the gang because they were part of the neighborhood and lived there. Even today that hasn't changed, the tradition of growing up in the neighborhood and associating promotes your desire in wanting to join. Because there are so many issues between neighborhoods you don't see members of other gangs joining or associating with your neighborhood. Back in the 50s and 60s there were guys from outside the area that were recruited into your neighborhood, because they hung out in the neighborhood.

I mentioned that there was no initiation process that an individual went through, but the homies made sure that you were not a flake and was able to fight and get down for the neighborhood and not run. Then there were those homies that didn't join the gang but belonged to the neighborhood.

Interviewer: Are/were any of your relatives in gangs?

Bono: Just like myself, there were other members of my family that grew up with gangs around the neighborhood. In those days, there were diverse types of gangs. You had the nice guys who were more of a social club; they had their cars that they worked on, and partied with their girls and friends.

Many of the social clubs that worked on their cars already had low riders, which they would drop to the ground and fix them all up, and paint them. Then there were the bad guys, those that were involved in violence, such as fighting, and stealing.

Interviewer: Why did you want to join the gang?

Bono: I got involved with these gangs because it was the thing to do in the 1950s. At that time, there were many gangs in the County of Los Angeles. To join a gang was the thing to do because there was nothing else, which was offered in the barrio.

Gang members already in their late 20s and early 30s had been involved in gang life for many years. The youth, including myself, we aspired to become a gang member because we saw others joining gangs, and we wanted to be recognized by those already involved in gangs who were the older leaders.

Interviewer: Does your parents know of your gang affiliation? How did they react to it?

Bono: Yes, my parents knew that I'm associated with the gang in my neighborhood. My mother didn't like it, but every time one of my homies wound up in juvenile hall or in jail, my dad would go down and get them out because he knew that if we were left in there we would get railroaded and wind up doing a lot of time for things we didn't commit.

Interviewer: Who started your gang?

Bono: I couldn't say who started the gang in the Colonia because there were older gang members who were known as the elders in them days. That gang had been formed years before. When I moved into Watts, the gangs there had already been established in the neighborhood. It is hard to say who started the gang in the beginning.

Interviewer: When did the gang begin?

Bono: I couldn't say when it began, I can only say that the older homies were there and they had been in the neighborhood gang for many years. In those days, I don't think that people cared to know who started the gang or when it began. Gangs were formed in all neighborhoods and the people joined them to be a part of them.

Interviewer: Why did the gang begin?

Bono: I believe that all gangs began to protect their neighborhood and that the members joined for protection from other gangs. As people moved into Los Angeles, gangs were formed to protect the new communities from the gangs, which were already there. Other gangs formed because they gave the young men something to do.

Interviewer: Does/did the gang have a leader?

Bono: Yes, all neighborhoods associated with gangs have leaders.

Interviewer: How was the leader selected?

Bono: Well, usually the toughest guy would be the leader of the gang, He was a man who was well liked because in those hays you had to earn the respect that was given to you. However, even though the leader, was the head of the gang, there were some members who wouldn't respect him. It was impossible for one man to control all the members of the gang. Some of the homies had their own followers and their own little groups and they would do their own thing.

Interviewer: What were the activities of your leader?

Bono: Speaking of the other rival gangs it was up to the leaders to gather the gang together and tell them want they would be doing. He would pass the word that we would be gathering at some ones' home, and meet at a certain time. If we were going to fight with one of our rivals, our leader would just say let's go and payback. No one would question, and he would plan how and when we would attack or spy on our enemies. He would not back down from anyone of anything. We would have parties and social gatherings together, which were planned by the leader.

Interviewer: What was the age range of the gang?

Bono: The gang ranged in age from 15 to the mid-20s, and then you had the older homies who were in their late 20s and early 30s, gang members broke away from all gang activities and got into selling drugs and supporting their habits. There were different group levels and as a member grew older he blended into one of those cliquas. But it was all according to how the person would conduct himself that he would be accepted in that clique. You had to earn the respect that was given to you.

Interviewer: Was there a female gang in the neighborhood?

Bono:	Back in the 50s and 60s there were female gangs. The females started having their leaders just like the homies in the neighborhood did. They would call themselves the Spiders, the Black Widows, and various other names to identify where they were from. They would dress in uniforms, using black blouses, or white, to identify the gang they belonged to. The female gang was an auxiliary to the males. They would party together and fight against other girls from other neighborhoods.
Interviewer:	What was the age range of the female gang members?
Bono:	They were between 15 and 22. Once they got married, they no longer participated in any gang activities because they were mothers and stayed at home.
Interviewer:	When did the female gangs begin?
Bono:	It's hard to say when they began, but I believe that they may have started back in the 40's. In the 1950's there were many females that were into gangs.
Interviewer:	What was the neighborhood life like or about?
Bono:	When I lived in La Colonia, the neighborhood was very poor. It all came to poverty; the kids didn't have anything to do. My dad worked at the racetrack and liked to gamble. There were days we ate meat and there were days all we had was the juice of the beans because the juice had a lot of protein. Keep in mind that a lot of the food that we ate we grew. Things like cilantro, chili, and vegetables among other things. One thing I can always give my mother credit, because she always managed to have food on the table.

Interviewer: Was your gang a fighting gang or a social gang?

Bono: The gang in my neighborhood was for the most part a social gang. We would kick in the neighborhood, drinking and just hanging around with each other. The only time we would fight was when another neighborhood came into our neighborhood and started something.

Interviewer: Would you explain how your gang recruited members into your gang or neighborhood?

Bono: Back then we did not have the kind of initiation that they have today to join a gang. Most of the members grew up in the neighborhood and was accepted into the gang because they hung out with the rest of the homies. Many times, people that joined the gang was because they had family members so that blended right in.

Interviewer: When did your gang use violence in their activities?

Bono: Violence only took place when there were serious issues. By this, I mean, if someone would rape, beat, steal from you or your family. If you were at dance and someone from another neighborhood want to pick up on your girlfriend that all hell would break loose. The violence wasn't that bad, but there was some.

Interviewer: Did your gang get involved in drugs?

Bono: There were those that were dealing drugs. Most of the homies smoked weed and then you had your heroin addicts. There were those that like downers, such as Quaaludes, reds, yellows, and Christmas trees. Neighborhoods didn't commit the crimes they commit today such as drive-bys, and shooting you just because you belonged to another neighborhood.

Interviewer: When did the police know that the gangs were dealing drugs?

Bono: Police always knew that there were illegal activities going on. They had their snitches and used them to buy drugs and do raids. Usually most of the gangsters went and scored with someone in the neighborhood because back then there was only a hand full of drug dealers around. It was pretty much controlled within the neighborhood even though marijuana and heroin came from Mexico. In today's market, we know that drugs are controlled by the cartel.

Interviewer: Do you feel or believe that drugs caused much of the violence?

Bono: Drugs was not the cause of violence back then. Most of the violence that took place would rise out of retaliation, vengeance, or just because a fight broke out at a party. Mostly everybody used drugs, such as whites also known as bennies, reds, or yellow jackets. Your heroin addicts didn't come around because they were doing their own thing. The only time that drugs were the cause of violence was when someone stole drugs from someone and they went after that individual. There were those as those like today that couldn't handle their drugs and got out of control, but that was far, few, and in between of that kind of violence.

Interviewer: What kind of weapons did the gang use to fight with?

Bono: There were very few weapons back then. Most of the weapons that were used were zip-guns or shotguns. Most of the time they fought with their fist, chains, or baseball bats. Usually when a gun was used was either to protect themselves or their families.

Interviewer: Why did your gang fight against other gangs?

Bono: Most of the time it was that we had nothing to do so after getting drunk we use to go to another neighborhood and raise hell. It was nothing like today that they fight over power or control of the drug world. Back then we did it just to have something to do. There were times that someone from another neighborhood would start something with someone from our neighborhood and then we would retaliate. Back then it was unlikely that several members of a gang would jump someone. It was nothing like today that you couldn't walk down the street without somebody hitting you up where you are from.

Interviewer: Would you explain the type of method of revenge that you would use?

Bono: Usually, the method I would personally use was my fist. When we had it out with another neighborhood there were times that we used chains, bats, brass knuckles. Seldom did you hear that a neighborhood would retaliate by coming in to your neighborhood and fire a gun, but it did happen.

Interviewer: How did the parents react when their son was a victim of gang violence?

Bono: Feelings or the feelings of people do not change when one of their love one is a victim. You must realize that my parents, just like your parents are human and they will feel hurt, sad, and angry all at the same time.

Interviewer: What does an older gang member do when they no longer are active in the gang?

Bono: There are those that continue to deal drugs, but for the most part they usually get married and move on with their lives. They try and raise a normal family like anyone else, but there is never any guarantee how the family is going to turn out no matter how hard you try. It's up to the individual and you cannot always put the blame on the neighborhood. These youngsters need to take responsibility for their actions.

Interviewer: Did they completely break away from gang activity?

Bono: First you need to realize that individuals will always be part of their neighborhood no matter what direction they take in life. Growing up in a poor community brings people together and they don't forget their experiences. Yes, the majority breaks away because they get married and become productive citizens. They further get involved with their kids hoping that they will not get involved in the gang as they did.

Interviewer: What happened to those who remained in the gang?

Bono: Those who remained involved continued their activity in the neighborhood, and either would wind up in prison, become winos, drug addicts, or wind up dead. The older homies are the ones younger homies would look up to for advice. Keep in mind that in today's generation the younger homies have no respect for no one including the veterano.

Interviewer: Do you know about the prison gangs?

Bono: Yes, gangs in prison is in many ways are different from the gangsters on the streets. The reason they are different is that most gangsters who are locked up are enemies on the outside. What I am saying by this is that outside everybody is in their own neighborhood, and in here they unite to survive the other gangs, for example in the South you have the EME which stands for the Mexican Mafia, and the North you have Nuestra Familia and both of this gangs are rivals. You also have the Surenios and this are the homies that represent the Southern California.

In prison, one needs to understand there is corruption on both sides, by this I mean with the inmates and the guards themselves. I am not at liberty to speak about the crimes that take place inside but believe me that there are guards that are worse than the inmates themselves and need to be part of the population. Inmates are not only discriminated they are dehumanized by the way they are treated. When I say that inmates are dehumanized one needs to look at the way inmates are incarcerated and kept in Pelican Bay.

Inmates that join gangs in prison many times join gangs for protection. The people that join gangs are usually individuals that are already active gang members on the streets. Keep this in mind and it will give an idea what prison is about, once those doors close behind there is no guarantee in what condition you will come out in. You may be turned out and by this, I mean you may become somebody's bitch, you may come out disabled, or you may come out with a tag on your toe.

Interviewer: As a parent do/did you encourage your children into gang activity?

Bono: Gangs was a way of life when I was growing up. I have always taught my children that to always stand up and let to one disrespect them or strip their rights from them. One thing that handed down to my kids is ethics, such being honest, to work hard, have respect and always have high respect for law enforcement.

My wife and I always stressed to our children that education is what will get them ahead in life. I taught my kids that no one could ever take away from them the knowledge that they would acquire in studying. One thing that most gang members do not want to see is their kids assume their role. For some reason people have this crazy idea that we are the ones that promote to have our kids join or become gang members, but that is a myth. My grandson started to get into trouble in school getting into activities that was not appropriate. I told my grandson that he would be sent to Iowa with his mother where they have zero tolerance for gang activity.

Interviewer: Are you still involved with gangs?

Bono: No, my entire outlook on life has changed and now I work towards reaching out not only to the young people in the neighborhood or the community, but I also work in reaching those who are still incarcerated. My goal is to try and help those who are released from prison to help them learn the process in getting their rights restored, and helping them realize that they too have rights, such as voting, going to school and so on.

Interviewer: Did you break away from gangs?

Bono: Yes and no, yes, I broke away from being active in the daily business of the gang. When I said no, it because I keep in touch with the neighborhoods in giving direction on how they can become productive citizens and how they can better their lives along with their families lives by investing in education and becoming role models in their communities. Getting involved is what this is about and making a difference in the community you live in.

Interviewer: Why did you break away from gangs?

Bono: If you take a good look around you and look at our communities, you can see that we have very limited resources in education, jobs, housing and health care. If I stayed in the gang it would have made no difference what part of the city I would have moved to. I learned many things in prison not knowing if I was going to spend the rest of my life there and there was no guarantee that I would walk out alive. So, I had a choice of staying in the same situation I was in as a youngster or I would have to change my ways if I were to make a difference.

Interviewer: What do you do now?

Bono: I am involved with several things in the community. I am a member and co-founder of the Adelante whose mission is helping inmates get their rights restored. I work with young individuals who need guidance and make them realize the importance of getting an education and school them on their rights. I speak at different engagements, I meet with families, individuals and groups and try to share my experiences in what I did wrong and how I have corrected my mistakes and not make them twice.

Interviewer: What does the gang do today?

Bono: The gang is still active in the neighborhood. The violence of course has gotten worse especially in this generation. Keep in mind that this is not only a new generation, but it is a different kind of breed. They have less respect not only for the parents but also for society in general.

Interviewer: What happen to the gang members in your generation?

Bono: Those that are alive are either settled down, others are in prison, and then you have those who have passed away. The ones that have settled down usually try and give the younger generation advice.

Interviewer: Do you believe there is more violence among gangs today?

Bono: Going back to the 60s gangs had more respect for authority than the gangs of today. Back in the days when I was growing up and through the 60s gangsters had respect for each other. For instance, say an individual had a score to settle with someone else, if the individual was strung out on drugs, the individual wanting to settle the score would allow the individual who was sick to get well before going after him. Today, these youngsters don't care, they will put a hit on you.

Weapons are more accessible today then back then. Today's gangsters have no morals and will hurt you just by you looking at them wrong. They will hurt you for no reason. There are neighborhoods that do get along those that don't, the reason being that they have a lot of issues among them. Drugs play a key role why the violence continues to rise.

Interviewer: Why do you believe that youth join gangs today?

Bono: There are several reasons why youth joins gangs. Reasons such as the ones we share with the public that they join gangs for protection, it could be that that they are not doing well in school. The economy for forces this individual motive to join gangs, because there are no jobs and their community has nothing to offer. Many times, in school kids are pushed aside for whatever reason and stereotyped as troublemakers. We need to put the blame on parents at times because we don't what their home life is like. Remember that there are many reasons why youth join gangs and you can't say that they join gangs for this one reason putting all the blame in the home.

Interviewer: What would you recommend that would help solve the gang problem in The County of Los Angeles?

Bono: Let's face it, the gang problem will never completely be resolved. I feel that we need to create jobs for our youth. We need to find better resources so that our kids can get a better education. By this

I mean if you compare the different communities throughout the County of Los Angeles. Take for example Roosevelt High School in Boyle Heights, they don't have the same resources that a school in Beverly Hills. There is no reason why our schools should be under this predicament, they should be able to give everyone the best education so that this kid can prepare for college. Programs that can motivate these young individuals too seek a better education. We need more programs both in prevention and intervention, communities to get involved and most of all we need to create jobs and have better resources to offer this kid if we are to make a difference.

Interviewer: Mr. Bono, is there anything else that you would like to share?

Bono: This letter that I wrote back in 1967 tells you how I really felt and what was/is happening to our people.

"It is the intention of this Court by this sentence to make sure that you are deprived from ever being free in society again."

My name is Victor Gerardo Bono, I'm 37 years of age, and have spent over half of my life in prison. I'm from Los Angeles, California, raised in the Watts area of that city in a little Chicano barrio we call "La Colonia" (The Colony), a predominately Chicano and Black ghetto "where our people (The working class) are socially, economically, and politically ostracized through generations of government neglect and have become surplus labor that is only sought after to fight the capitalist wars and fill prisons. I have been a prisoner in federal custody for the last nine years sentenced as mentioned to spend the rest of my life, to be an incarcerated slave. A life that we vigorously resist. Since my incarceration (1958), I've struggled to reach and raise the level of conciseness of the brothers that I meet in the various federal prisons, as I'm continually transferred from one prison to another because of such efforts. I've been involved with the founding of four Marxist-Leninist Study Collectives; participated in the development of the Chicano Culture Study Groups; written many critical articles relating to the federal prison system, and federal government; about constitutional violations. I believe in organization, and organizational efforts in combating the government with its two types of justice system.

In simple terms, collective struggle in my view, is one of the answers to our situation, and the other is that of dedicated support from our committed friends and comrade outside in the communities. Experience has been a good teacher to us, and in the other hand, it has been precisely that experience of the government that has allowed this Control Unit to be a reality unchecked, and to be hidden for so long from public scrutiny. I believe that it will be the efforts and struggle of a United Front to stop this evil monster from growing any more in kind. I have devoted my time to the study of Marxist-Leninist principles, because of my attentive interest in this subject and support of the ideology, I have been labeled as a threat to the security in the various federal penitentiaries (Concentration Camps) by the prison administrations. As a result, I have been brought forcibly to the infamous Control Unit Treatment Program at Marion, Illinois.

Having spent a total of two and a half years in this behavioral modification laboratory type fortress, I have witnessed atrocities that are on the same par as Pinochets' Concentration Camps in Chile, and that of Hitlers' Auschwitz. It is important that the public at large be made aware of what their tax dollars are being used for at this facility. The Control Unit should be closed not only because of what it does to us prisoners that are force into it, but for what it represents in term of oppression, repression, and suppression of human rights to all subjected to it. The Unit has profoundly affected our thinking, the realization of the lengths the federal government will go in their psychological and physical tortures-the striving to reduce and destroy our wills to resist-with the use of sensory deprivation, long term and indefinite confinement. It is my true belief by voice of what I have seen that the wheels of oppression are set to destroy our minds in here, set on driving us to destroy ourselves by this program. We know this is the case in what happened to Jackson "Curley" Tee, Paul X. Duhart, Willy "Gypsy" Adams, and just recently LeCount Bly, these brothers are all dead because of this Unit. We have faith in the people outside, I'm sure they will help and support our struggle, for it's a just cause.

Oral Interview #2

The interviewee was "Huero Waldo", a retired gang member and veterano from Big Hazard, now a volunteer with the community and doing outreach and intervention work, he has a lot to offer from his experience. Most of his life he was involved with gang activity in the neighborhood where he grew up in the Los Angeles housing project known as Ramona Gardens.

Interviewer: Are you/were you a gang member?

"Huero": I consider myself a retired gang member who still goes back to the community and so outreach work. There was a time that I was active in the neighborhood, to answer your question yes at once upon a time I was considered a gang member.

Interviewer: When did you begin your association with gangs?

"Huero": I started hanging around with the homies in the neighborhood about the age of 16. Everybody knew each other and we just hung around and became part of the neighborhood.

Interviewer: How old were you when you became a gang member?

"Huero": I was about 16 years of age.

The Way Out

Interviewer: Are/were any of your relatives in gangs?

"Huero": Yes.

Interviewer: Why did you want to join the gang?

"Huero": It wasn't that I wanted to join a gang, it just happened, that was being part of the neighborhood. You need to understand that growing up in the projects they automatically stereotype you as a gang member. Another way of looking at it is you go to school with certain individuals and that is how cliques get started.

Interviewer: Did your parents know of your gang affiliation? How did they react to it?

"Huero": Yes, my parents knew I hung around in the neighborhood, but they always gave me advice not to do unlawful things that would make me wind up in jail. They always taught me to defend myself if someone wanted to fight, but they also told me to try and avoid any problems that came my way. One thing that I can say positive about my parents, they always taught us to be honest, hardworking, and respect our elders.

Interviewer: Who started the gang?

"Huero": No one really knows who started the gang. It's like I said before that youngsters hang around together and before you know it, they are stereotyped as gang members. Way back when the neighborhood came together, they came together for protection from other neighborhoods.

Interviewer: When did your gang begin?

"Huero": Like I said before, that the neighborhood was there before I came along.

Interviewer: Why did the gang begin?

"Huero": The neighborhood came together for protection from outsiders and other cultures that were a threat to our people. You must understand that all lives we had been discriminated, not only job wise but in schools and everywhere we turned around, because of the color of our skin.

Interviewer: Does the gang have a leader?

"Huero": Not necessarily a leader, we looked up to the older homies that were examples to us. They were the ones that gave us advice, and many times kept us out of trouble.

Interviewer: How was the leader selected?

"Huero": The individuals that ran the neighborhood, were individuals that everyone respected and liked. They were the ones that had a good head on their shoulders. They didn't want any of us to get into trouble or get hurt.

Interviewer: What were the activities of your leader?

"Huero": The homies that ran the neighborhood made sure that everyone got along. That no one would take advantage of someone that was weak or someone that lived in the neighborhood and didn't hang around or wasn't part of the gang. These individuals would be the ones that planned the parties and spread the word around about the party. They made sure that we were prepared if outsiders or troublemakers came wanting to start trouble. We didn't use guns unless someone else came in shooting at us. Then that's when guns were pulled; other than that, we had no reason to be violent in that way. Other activities that the older homies would get us involved in were carwashes, picnics, we played baseball together and other sports.

Interviewer: What was the age range of the gang?

"Huero": The ages were between 16 through 24, very seldom did you see anybody younger than that hanging around the older homies.

Interviewer: Were there female gangs in the neighborhood?

"Huero": There were a few, the majority that hung out with the homies were their girlfriends. If they had to get down they would, but mostly they would cater to their boyfriends. Women back then weren't really known for gang activity.

Interviewer: What was/is the neighborhood life?

"Huero": Life in the projects is very poor, and resources are limited. Let me start by telling you that first we live in a place ran by the County of Los Angeles, and when the cops see the youngsters hanging out they assume that they are taking part in gang activity. "Big Hazard" is known as one of the most unique neighborhoods in the County of Los Angeles. Going back to the fifties and sixties, I remember how the cops had already stereotyped us as gang members. They used to harass us just for hanging out in the neighborhood.

Many of the people living in the projects are on some type of assistance, either County or State, and are limited on funds. There are those people that have jobs and rent according to their income. Families in the neighborhood try to raise their kids in a respectful way; it's us that go the wrong way and, no one can blame our parents for our mistakes.

People in the neighborhood are just like anybody else anywhere. Many of the parents teach their kids to be honest, get an education, and go to work. There are families that are single parents and struggle to bring up their kids, but they try and lead them the right way. We all know that there are individuals that never learn and continue to break the law, by stealing, selling drugs or being deviant.

Interviewer: Was your gang a fighting gang or a social group?

"Huero": Well, in the projects there isn't many ways of coming in or getting out without being noticed. To answer your question, I consider my neighborhood both a fighting and social neighborhood. Everybody kicks it in the project and we partied in the parking lot or in somebody's apartment. If someone came in looking for trouble they would find someone to grant them their wish.

Interviewer: Would you explain how your gang recruited members?

"Huero": Everybody new everybody in the neighborhood. We all hung out at the teen center and kicked it. Back then there was no initiation, either you found your place with the homies you hung out with or they had other family members who were gang members. Other ways they recruited was the individual that wanted to join the gang would be asked to go into another neighborhood and start a fight and then the rest of the homies would back up the individual. Most of the members joined because they were part of the family.

Interviewer: When did your gang use violence in their activities?

"Huero": The only time we used violence was when there were real serious issues, such as someone jumping and hurting a family member, or a member from the neighborhood. Weapons weren't used unless someone shot someone in the neighborhood or something serious happened. Back then and as far as the sixties, it was hard to get guns. We made Zip guns and fought with knives or chains.

Interviewer: Did your gang get involved with drugs?

"Huero": Yes, there were those that sold drugs in the neighborhood, but to say that we got involved with drugs, as far as selling "no", as far as using "yes".

Interviewer: Do you believe that the drugs caused more violence?

"Huero": Not really, because we mostly smoked weed, and took some whites (bennies), reds, and so on. You had your heroin addicts back then, but they hung around mostly among themselves. We didn't have the kinds of drugs in the neighborhood like they have today.

Interviewer: What did the gang use?

"Huero": Mostly our fists, very rarely did we use knives, or chains, and very seldom did we use a gun. Times have changed, homie, we didn't even come close to these gangsters of today with the kind of arsenal that is made available today.

Interviewer: Why did your gang fight against other gangs?

"Huero": There were many reasons why we fought with other neighborhoods. It depended on the reason what came down. For instance, there were times we went to another neighborhood just because we got a wild hair up our you know what. Other time there might have been a reason, such as someone from another neighborhood jumping one of our homies. Back then most of the neighborhoods had respect for each other even if you partied in their neighborhood, no one really tripped where you were from.

There were times we fought with our rivals when they came cruising through our neighborhood and acting stupid, for instance when they came in tagging in our neighborhood and writing all over our walls. Violence as we know it today didn't happen that way when I was growing.

Interviewer: Would you explain the method of revenge that you used?

"Huero": Most of the time nothing was planned or premeditated. Everybody would mostly do their own thing. There were diverse groups that would hang around with each other. Usually you had two three guys just kicking it. There were various kinds of problems, such as having someone that was weak, but didn't want to get involved in the activity of the gang, but wanted to hang around them. We usually would take care of the problem ourselves making sure that the individual understood what he had to do if he wanted to hang with the homies.

Then you had the homies that no one in the neighborhood would mess with because of their reputation. There were the non-fighters, and then you had the homies that would get down by a drop of a hat. The worst revenge involved someone being shot or being killed. Many times, these individuals would act stupid and get themselves hurt. Other times, there were serious issues and that's when violence would occur.

As I mentioned before, there was very little violence and mostly the retaliation that was used was fighting with your fists, at times with chains and knives. Very seldom was a weapon used. We either fought for the hell of it, or to show another neighborhood that we could hold our own.

Interviewer: How did your rivals react to your retaliation?

"Huero": Back then we thought we were bad and thought that we really took care of business. The truth of the matter is, that we were gentle giants compared to the gangsters of today. Fighting would go on for days, but usually we would squash the fighting after about two or three days. Even after the retaliation would take place, people from different neighborhoods would get along.

Interviewer: How did the parents react when their son/daughter was a victim of gang violence?

"Huero": Parents have always had the habit of putting the blame on someone else other than their kid, I guess that's only natural. Just like today, back then parents were in denial that their kids were involved in gang activity. The entire group was blamed because those parents believed that we would force their sons to get involved in gang activities, violent activity or to steal and take drugs.

Then there were those families that accepted that their sons or daughters were involved on their own accord. Other parents accepted that their loved one was a victim of a horrible crime. They know that something like this could happen to anyone. We have always stuck together and give our condolences to the families that lose someone. Somehow, or some way we try and raise money to help the families that lose someone to violence.

Interviewer: What did the older gang member do, who no longer got involved in violent activity?

"Huero": In the neighborhood, the older members stop getting involved in gang activity as they get older, somewhere in their twenties. Some get married leading a productive life. They go to work and start having kids, which makes them aware that now they have a responsibility to their family. Most of the time they don't forget where they came from and they in return try and give the younger homies advice about what they face daily if they continue to be involved with the gang.

Interviewer: Did they break away completely from gang activity?

"Huero": Yes, for the most part. You have those that continued selling marijuana, but got away from the violence.

Interviewer: What happened to those who remained involved?

"Huero": Some of them ended up in jail or prison. Others get involved in more serious crimes and then there are those that seek religion and make that change. Those that are in prison for the most part just want to do their time and get out.

Interviewer: What do you see now?

"Huero": That depends on what you mean by what I see now. I see a generation that we need to reach before they destroy themselves. We need to try and get these youngsters turned around. The only way that we will turn youngsters around is by creating jobs that pay a decent wage, and send them to school to get an education or some type of trade.

Interviewer: Why did you break from gangs?

"Huero": I came to realize that being involved with the gang has a lot of negative outcomes, such as getting arrested and going to jail, winding up dead or crippled among other things. I thought that gang life was happening. After a while, you get burned out, and you realize that there are more productive things one can do in life. But let me say this that we never forget where we came from. Life in the neighborhood starts out innocent by just hanging out and partying. Before you know it, you find yourself caught up in the web of gang life.

As I mentioned earlier, I was tired of parting, and hanging out. I got married and came to realize that I now had other responsibilities and that I needed to take the responsibility of raising a family. I still drank and partied, but as the years went by we started having kids and somehow that's what made me change. You see, marriage has magic, it makes you grow up suddenly, and that's when you start making your parents proud, because that's when your mother tells you that her prayers were answered.

I needed to make a change and find something different than partying and taking drugs, because we all know that drugs influence your health. I've seen many of my homies become diabetics, get hepatitis c and even see some pass away from cirrhosis of the liver among other sickness. I guess the older you get the wiser you become, because you realize the effects or the odds you are up against. I wanted to do more than just hang around. I instead speak to the younger homies that were growing up and try to make them realize what happens when you continue to party and take drugs. I tell them that it is important for them to go to school and get a trade, or go to college and become a voice for their people. My goal now is to continue working with the homies in the neighborhood and try to shift their way of thinking.

Interviewer: What does the gang do today?

"Huero": The neighborhood is still around and has a history sating back to the 1920s. There are different cliques in the neighborhood, and they have their own program going on. You have those that retired from gang activity and then you have those that are still active. For the most part I don't get involved with the activity that takes place in the neighborhood. Most of the veteranos live and let live, and when they can

	they talk to the younger homies to have respect for the older homies, which doesn't always happen.
Interviewer:	What happens to the members?
"Huero":	Just as I said before, the majority are married and settled down. There are those who have passed away or died behind violence. Then you have those that are in prison for a long time for the crimes they committed.
Interviewer:	Do you believe there is more violence among gangs today?
"Huero":	Of course, there is much more violence today than when I was growing up. You must realize that we didn't have the armor that they have in today's world. When I was growing up we had shotguns, a hand gun occasionally, but mostly we used chains, knives, and zip guns we used we made ourselves, they were called zip-guns. When you read the paper, you see the kind of weapons these youngsters use today, such as semi-automatic weapons, hi-caliber rifles that can knock an elephant down, so the answer to your question is yes, violence is greater today than ever before.
Interviewer:	What do you believe is the reason that youth join gangs?
"Huero":	Gang life is the way of life for many individuals in the neighborhood. The older homies retire, and the younger ones take over the neighborhood. One of the reasons that youth join gangs is because there are really no opportunities for our youth today. It is like it was back when I was growing up. There are

no mobs, kids get pushed aside in the schools or class room and degraded by being told that college is too hard and they should take classes such as auto mechanics or a wood working class, because they truly aren't college material. Gangs gives young individuals the opportunity of making money that otherwise they wouldn't make. You must realize that the neighborhood gives these youngsters opportunities that no one else gives them.

"Huero": Are younger youth getting involved in the gangs?

Interviewer: Yes, you now have youth joining gangs as young as eleven years old and sometimes even at a younger age.: Youth are getting recruited into gangs at a very much younger age, not only in the neighborhood but at the schools as well.

"Huero": How do you feel about youth joining gangs?

Interviewer: I feel bad, because I feel that the government can do more for these kids to lead a better life. We know that these youngsters have the habit of not listening to anybody because they think they know it all. Regardless of they think, we need to offer these youths something other than hardships if we are going to take control on the gang problem that our communities face.

"Huero": What would you recommend to help solve the gang problem in the County of Los Angeles?

"Huero": The government should help provide not only jobs for those youth that drop out of school, but provide summer jobs for students that are eligible to work. We have so many youths that want to go to school, but because they are in schools with limited resources, or where violence is common, or it is drug infested, they fear for their well-being and survival. This alone can stress someone out and make them just want to get out from the situation.

Much more needs to be done for the single parents who are on some kind of assistance. More help needs to be given so they could have relief from having to pay for things that they cannot afford to give their kids. We know that there are those that use the money they get to do drugs and drink, but it would help bring reduction to the problem. If we had programs that could reach out to our youth and give them something positive, this within itself would curb violence and some gang activity.

Interviewer: "Huero", is there anything else you would like to share?

"Huero": I would like to close by saying, that if we all got involved in helping our youth today there is so much that can be done to help our youth turn around. It doesn't matter if you just live in the community, or belong to a church, the idea is to get involved to make a difference.

Chapter 6

Summary, Solutions, and Suggestions Proposed for Further Research and Conclusion

THE GANG PHENOMENON IS a major concern in the United States today as youth fight each other and victimize innocent people. The cost of law enforcement involved in dealing with gangs, investigating their crimes, and protecting the community is tremendous. In Los Angeles County, problems with juvenile gangs have continued to mount, particularly in the disadvantaged sections of the cities where the gangs have taken control of neighborhood schools and recreational facilities. Today, gangs gave spread from central Los Angeles to every city of the county. In 2003, Los Angeles tops the list with close to 8,000 gangs and 300,000 gang members, about 80% of which were identified as Chicano/Latino, including all gang members from the different Latino cultures from other countries.

The neighborhood is very important to the gang member; it is where he/she lives and bands together with others. Members of the gang identify with their territory and feel a great deal of pride in it. The graffiti which one Chicano/Latino gang writes on the wall clearly marks the boundary of their neighborhood. This warfare is carried on by youth who perceive themselves as "soldiers defending their home."

Life within the neighborhood often revolves around the gang and its activities. The gang offers opportunities that a youth does not receive at home or at school. Gang affiliation fulfills certain basic needs such as self-esteem, a sense of identity, prestige, a sense of belonging, protection, and something to do. Chicano/Latino youth often do not find these needs met either in their families or in the dominant society. It is reasonable to hypothesize that by their violence, these youths are reacting to the long history of discrimination and prejudice against Chicano/Latino Americans. The origins of these prejudices can be traced back to 1848 when the Southwest Territories were annexed to the United States. We have also seen the evolution of neighborhoods, in part, as a response to these prejudices. The first neighborhood in Los Angeles, Sonoratown, emerged as a separate community of Chicanos/Latinos during Anglo society. When new Mexican immigrants arrived in Los Angeles, they sought Sonoratown as a place to live-a familiar place. Thus, the Chicano/Latino population increased in Sonoratown. Chicano/Latino Americans who had lived in Sonoratown for a long time moved to outlying areas of the city and county. East Los Angeles and South Los Angeles along Alameda Street were the next areas of the county to be populated by Chicanos/Latinos. Subsequently, as new immigrants continued to arrive in Los Angeles, the long-term Chicano/Latino residents moved further into the suburbs leaving the older neighborhoods for the new immigrants who had few economic resources. In this way, the neighborhoods continued to increase in numbers throughout Los Angeles County from as early as the 1880s when residents began to leave Sonoratown. The growth in numbers of neighborhoods roughly parallels the rise in numbers of the Chicano/Latino population in Los Angeles County.

The large body of research of the 15 to 20 years has been undertaken to achieve an understanding and a hope for providing a solution to the problem to violent gangs. Yet, not everyone understands the gang phenomenon in the same fashion as one who has lived or lives in the neighborhood. Besides adding to the literature on gangs, the researcher has provided information for a better understanding of Chicano/Latino gangs and their historical development. An explanation is offered for the evolution of neighborhoods and their relationship to the increase in number of Chicano/Latino gangs. Some reasons why Chicano/Latino youth join gangs today have been presented.

The findings in this study support other studies of ethnic gangs in general, while at the same time contributing to the literature on the development of Chicano/Latino gangs. Among those who could benefit from this study are (a) other researchers who are trying to understand gangs in order to offer a solution to their violence; (b) historians who desire to explore more about the history of Chicano/Latino gangs and their development, since there are few documented studies on this subject; (c) government agencies such as sheriff's departments, police departments, and correctional agencies (e.g. California Youth Authority), who are constantly confronted with gangs and their violence; (d) community organizations such as schools where gangs tend to proliferate, recruit, gather, and commit violence; and (e) the Chicano/Latino community and gang members themselves who want to know the history of the development of gangs and the extent of their violence.

Society may benefit from this study by understanding the historical development of Chicano/Latino population in the Southwest and the evolution of Chicano/Latino gangs in the city, county, or state. Gaining knowledge of the development of the Chicano/Latino community will provide understanding of the gang neighborhood, why gangs are formed, why youth continue to join gangs, and why they are still increasing in numbers and violence.

The findings of this study uphold the observations of other researchers by demonstrating similar characteristics, or parallels, whether they are drawn from gangs in the 1830s, 1880s, 1920s, or 2000s. For example, Irish gangs in the 1830s joined together in the face of poverty, isolation, and great prejudice just as we have seen with Chicano/Latino gangs. Thrasher (1963) found most Chicago gangs were in the slums or poverty sections of the city. Chicano/Latino gangs share with these earlier gangs the poverty of the slum environment.

Ethnic gangs throughout history have been notorious for violent behavior. Gangs fought to maintain their territory in the city much the same way that Chicano/Latino gangs fight to maintain their territory. Violent feuds resulted as rivals would brawl on the streets and challenge others in the historic gangs in early United States history as well as modern Chicano/Latino gangs. Law enforcement agencies have witnessed the rapid escalation of violent, gang-related activity of modern Chicano/Latino gangs directed against rival gangs and the public. The challenges of rival gangs today lead to open war and much violence. For instance, the extent of violence is seen in the number of related homicides, 503 from January 2003 to December 2003. This included non-gang related homicides, including innocent bystanders who were victims of violent shootings.

Results from this study and previous studies presented here show further parallels between ethnic gangs:

1. Youth join gangs with the direct or tacit approval of their parents.
2. Youth can achieve a sense of identity, bravado, and a sense of respect by becoming part of the neighborhood gang.
3. Identification with the gang is maintained generation after generation, even to the present day.
4. Gang members are willing to fight, even die, for their neighborhood.
5. Adolescents interpret the gang as the only group, which provides positive feedback such as feeling of belonging, and the recognition of being someone. They can express themselves by their participation in gangs.
6. The gang thus replaces the family by satisfying the basic needs for growing adolescents.

In addition, another parallel which can be identified among ethnic gangs is the transition from violent gang activity by older gang members to young adult life. The older members usually drop out of the violent activities to rear children establish a family life. Many maintain communication with their gang in an advisory role, or to participate in less violent activities of the gang, such as drugs. Those are a common pattern among modern Chicano/Latino gangs in Los Angeles.

Finally, other parallels to be found among ethnic gangs, including Chicano/Latino gangs, are: (a) gang members and Chicano/Latino youth have poor models, (b) the gang is involved with drugs, and (c) the gang is involved in illegal activities. These are crucial factors in delinquent causation among gangs. This study demonstrates the many parallels among ethnic gangs. It also points to the need for further work in the field since neither police crackdowns nor short-term political projects have provided a solution to gangs. The gang problem remains a serious community problem. Progress in dealing with it can only be made when the community-at-large, at the political and economic level, becomes involved.

Suggestions for Further Research

1. Future studies should investigate the population of children in gang neighborhoods who do not become delinquents and determine what types of coping/adapting mechanisms allow these individuals to lead lives free of violence and crime.

2. This study should be replicated with a larger sample of interviews in different areas of the county to substantiate the data gathered.

3. Studies should be situated to investigate the educational surrounding of youth to determine (a) why youth fail to continue their education, (b) why youth are being recruited into gangs at a much younger age, and (c) the impact of gangs in the schools.

4. Future historians should continue to develop the background of information on gangs to provide further insights into the gangs and their formation.

Government and law enforcement agency gang units, such as the Los Angeles County Sheriff's Department Operations Unit (OSS), should be interviewed to elucidate questions and concerns which have arisen in this study. Government researchers may have insights, which quite possibly could lead to a solution to the violence of ethnic gangs, especially the Chicano/Latino gangs in the County of Los Angeles.

Solutions

Social scientists and criminologists agree that intervention and prevention are the best methods of dealing with gangs (Conley, 1993). California school districts have made it a part of their agenda to ask what to do about gangs and gang activity. Providing safer schools and a better education are high on the list of priorities for California school districts.

Lasley (1992) asserted that gang members rarely graduate from high school. Blame tends to be directed toward the student, and rarely toward the school system. In addition, when a son-gang member drops out of school, the blame in usually pointed toward a gang member. Teachers sway students into taking easier courses and urge them to attend trade schools instead of taking the courses that are required to admission to a college or university.

Children that speak Spanish are kept in Limited English Proficient (LEP) categories. Interestingly, school districts receive twice the financial resources for LEP students as they do for mainstream students. Their social and academic interactions as well as their English-speaking skills are often adequate; yet these students have been denied transition into regular classes (Boyle, 1996).

Accentuating the way society respects the humanity of all people can be a resource when communication between students and teachers fail (Hallcom, 1993). Special education programs should be mandated to find methods of teaching and counseling antisocial students with behavioral problems (Lewis, 1007). For those that seek peer approval and recognition, a special place may be needed to separate them from those students who want to go to school to learn and behave appropriately.

Aiming early intervention, the program known as Pursuing Academic Choices Together (PACT) seeks to enhance parents' sense of responsibility, participation, obligation, and awareness. To reach out to youth before they join gangs is the purpose of this program. Most researchers indicate that increasing juvenile self-esteem is a helpful tool in keeping children out of gangs (all own, 1993).

In 1983, the Los Angeles Police Department along with the Los Angeles Unified School district developed the Drug Abuse Resistance Education Program (DARE) aimed at fifth, sixth, and seventh graders. Their goal has been to help youths say "no".

Citizens and religious groups are doing much work in prevention, as well as intervention, with the help of former gang members, who assist citizens to formulate creative solutions. While there may be no single solution to gang problems, groups like this can make a difference. Additional resources, such as community mobilization, social intervention involving counseling, tutoring, and many other resources provide opportunities including job assistance and recreational program. (The most successful programs have the following common characteristics (Silverman, 1994):

> ➢ Large numbers of sponsors, both public and private.
> ➢ Involvement of police and community service agencies.
> ➢ An outreach component composed of at-risk youth.
> ➢ Availability of a variety of services such as counseling, positive life experiences, and productive goals.

Gilbert M. Griñie

Prevention

Prevention is a key to controlling gang activity. To help youths turn away from gangs and gang activities, we need to intervene and minimize the difference those individuals and individuals who try to instill fear on others. Strong, highly motivating education and training programs are needed to help at-risk youth to become more productive and responsible.

Trustworthiness, respect, responsibility, fairness, caring, and citizenship are values that comprise a core ethics that needs to be taught in the home, and be reinforced within in the classroom (Josephson Institute, 2000). These values serve as a guide for individuals in making appropriate decisions.

Gang members who come from homes where there is no nurturing are likely to show signs of poor self-esteem and, in many cases, cause problems in the classroom. Alternatives to gang programs are needed in addition to counseling, such as job training, jobs, and educational support to help at-risk youth lead more positive creative lives (Spergel, 1992). Living in poverty, at-risk youth may find it difficult to meet basic physical and psychological needs, leading to a lack of self-esteem and pride. The family and community may help most at-risk children succeed in life through protective factors and unexpected sources of support (Rak & Patterson, 1996). Research that explains the relationship between gang members and juvenile delinquency is limited (Thornberry, 1993). Schools and communities can limit gang membership through the type of services provided. According to Garbarino (1995), one must capitalize on the strength of our youth by teaching them coping skills and providing them with a forum where their accomplishments can be felt, and setting goals for the future that can be reached. Schools and teachers who are capable of teaching and discussing situational ethics can contribute toward gang prevention.

Teachers experiencing higher levels of stress due to an increase in workloads and violence in schools, need proper training and awareness of gangs and gang activities. Parents and educators who suspect gang activity should talk to the youth and report their concerns to school officials and counselors to secure help for these individuals. School-based prevention programs must begin in a child's early education and stress the importance of building a relationship of trust between student and teacher.

Conclusion

A variety of factors contribute to gang affiliation and according to social learning theory, individuals acquire certain behaviors and attitudes such as, "I don't need you" or "I'm bad; don't mess with me if you know what's good for you" Akers, 1985). The fact that more and more youth are joining gangs at a much younger age and that they are more violent suggests that teachers needs to become even more aware of gangs and gang activities.

Administrators must be realistic in their approach to gangs and their efforts to prevent or reduce gang activities. School officials must believe that nothing is more important than providing a safe-earning environment for students and staff by confronting and marginalizing all gang activities.

It is necessary to review academic progress, attendance patterns, and disciplinary records to document gang membership. Youth that are experiencing difficulties with their classes, tutoring, or homework may want to select and alternative education program.

There is no easy resolution or approach to preventing gang participation. If we expect youths to become people of character, trustworthy, respectful, responsible, fair, caring, and good citizens, then these six pillars of character need to be instilled in the homes as well as in the classrooms throughout their lives. Allowing the educator to reach children as an early age and to continue to assist them through the teen years will reduce the likelihood of involvement in gangs and overall gang activity.

References

Acuña, R. (1972). *Occupied America: The Chicano's Struggle Toward Liberation*. San Francisco: Canfield.

Adler, P., Hocevar, D., & Ovando, C. (1984). *Familiar Correlates of Gang Membership: An Exploratory Study of Mexican American Youth*. Hispanic Journal of Behavioral Science, 6, (1), 65-76.

Akers, R. L. (1985). *Deviant Behavior: A Social Learning Approach* (3rd ed). Belmont CA, Wadsworth

Alonzo, A. A. (1999). *Territoriality Among African-American Street Gangs in Los Angeles*. Maters Thesis, present to the University of Southern California.

Altarriba, J., & Bauer, L. M. (1998). *Counseling the Hispanic Client: Cuban Americans, Mexican Americans, and Puerto Ricans*. Journal of Counseling & Development. 76. 389-395.

Baker, B. (1988). *Modern Gangs Have Roots in Racial Turmoil of '60s*. Los Angeles Times June 26, pB28, 31.

Bandura, A. (1976). *Analysis of Delinquency and Aggression*. Lawrence Associates, INC: New Jersey

Bloch, B. (1958). *The Gang: A Study in Adolescent Behavior*. New York: Philosophical Library.

Bogardus, E. S. (1926). *The City Boy and His Problems: A Survey of Boy Life in Los Angeles*. Los Angeles. House of Ralston, Rotary Club of Los Angeles.

Bond, J. Max. (1936). *The Negro in Los Angeles*. Unpublished Dissertation, University of Southern California

Boyle, G. Dolores Mission Proyecto, director of "Jobs for the Future" September 18, 1996. [Viedo]. Los Angeles, CA and E Home Video Firm.

Brownstein, A. (2000). *Gangs*, Available at: www.streetgangs.com.

Bunch, L. G. (1990). "A Past Not Necessarily Prologue: the Afro-American in Los Angeles Since 1900." *In 20 Century Los Angeles: Power, Promotion, and Social Conflict*, edited by Norman M. Klein and Martin J. Schiesl, 22-48. Claremont, Calif.: Regina Books.

Burrell, M (1984, March 15). *4 Gangs Talk to Cope, One Another*. Independent Press-Telegram (Long Beach, California), Sec. B, pp. 1, 2.

California. Office of the Attorney General, Youth Gang Task Force, (1981). *Report on Youth Gang Violence in California*. Sacramento: State Printing Office.

Campbell, A. (1987). "Self-Definition by Rejection: The Case of Gang Girls." *Social Problems*, 34 (5) December: 451-466.

Castro, T. (1974). *Chicano Power: The Emergence of Mexican America*. New York: Saturday Review Press.

Cervantes, R. C., Castro, F. G. (1985). *Stress, Coping, and Mexican American Mental Health: A Systematic Review*. Hispanic Journal of Behavior Science, 7, 1-3

Chavez, J. (2001). Still Separate, Still Unequal: A look at racial inequality in California Schools 47 Years After Brown. versus Board of Education. California for Justice Educational Foundation, volume 2, 1-28.

Chin, Ko-lin (1990). "Chinese Gangs and Extortion." in Huff, C. Ronald (ed) (1990) *Gangs in America*. Newbury Park: Sage.

Cloward, R., & Ohilin, L, (1960). *Delinquency and opportunity: A Theory of Delinquent gangs*. Glencoe, IL: The Free Press.

Collins, K. E. (1980). *Black Los Angeles: The Maturing of the Ghetto, 1940-1950*. Saratoga, Calif.: Century Twenty-One Publishing.

Conley, C. H., (1993). *Street Gangs Current Knowledge and Strategies*. Washington, DC: Institute of Justice.

Corson, B. L., (1981). *An Interview Study of 40 Juvenile Hispanic Gang Students*. Unpublished master's thesis, California State University, Long Beach.

Davis, M. (1990). *City of Quartz: Excavating the Future in Los Angeles*. New York: Vintage Press.

Dworkin, A. G., (1983). A city founded, a people lost. In L. I. Duran & H. Bernard (Eds.), *Introduction to Chicano studies* (pp. 445-449). New York: Macmillan.

Erlanger. H. S. (1982). *Estrangement, Machismo, and Gang Violence*. In L.D. Savitz & N. Johnston (Eds.), Contemporary criminology (pp/ 184-194). New York: Wiley & Sons.

Furillo, A. (1983, November28). *Tradition Turns to Violence as Members Play by New Rules*. Los Angeles Herald Examiner, Sec. A, pp. 1, 8, 9.

Garbarino, J, (1995). *The American War Zone: What Children Can Tell Us About Living with Violence*. Journal of Developmental and Behavioral Pediatrics, 16(6), 431-435

Gale Encyclopedia of Childhood & Adolescence, (1998). Gangs. Gale Research Available: www.finarticles.com

Garraty, J. A. (1979). *The American Nation: A History of the United States Since 1965* (Vol. 2, 4th ed.). New York: Harper & Row.

Gedatus, G. (2000). *Gangs and Violence*. Calpstone Press. Mankato, Minnesota.

Greenan, S., Britz, M., Rush, J., & Baker, T. (2000). *Gangs: An International Approach*. New Jersey, N. J.: Prentice Hall Inc.

Griswold del Castillo, R, (1979). *The Los Angeles Barrio, 1850-1890*. Berkeley: University of California Press.

Hallcom, F. G., (1993). *Single Mothers in the Los Angeles Latino Community: A Developing Underclass*. In Gender, Self and Society ed. Renate Von Bardeleben NY: Peter Lang Publishers, Hinds, M. H. (2001, May 18).

Haskins, K. (1974). *Street Gangs: Yesterday and Today*. New York: Haskins Haskins Publishing House.

Howell, J. C., Krisberg, B, Hawkins, K.D., & Wilson, J. J. (Eds.) (1995). *Serious, Violent, and Chronic Juvenile Offenders: A Sourcebook*. Thousand Oaks, CA: Sage Publications.

Ibrahim, F. A. (1991). *Contribution of Cultural Worldview to Generic Counseling and Development*. Journal of Counseling and Development, 70, 13-19

Josephson Institute. (2000). *The Six Pillars of Character*. Retrieved November 21, 2000. from http://www.charactercounts.org/defsix.htm.

Juvenile Justice Clearinghouse (1995). *Draft report on Stage 1 assessment, National Youth Gang Suppression and Intervention Program*. Rockville, MD: Author.

Kenney, J. P., Pursuit, D. G. Fuller, D. E., & Barry, R. F. (1982). *Police Work with Juveniles and the Administration of Juvenile Justice* (6th ed.). Springfeild, IL. Charles V. Thomas.

Klein, M. W. (1977). *Street Gangs and Street Workers*. Englewood Cliffs, NJ: Prentice-Hall.

Kramer, D., & Kramer < (1953). *Teen-age Gangs*. New York: Henry Holt.

Kontos, etc, Gangs and Society. NY, Columbia University Press, 2003.

Lamb, R. S. (1970). *Mexican Americans: Sons of the Southwest*. Claremont, CA: Ocelot Press.

Lapp, R. M. (1987). *Afro-Americans in California.* 2nd ed. San Francisco: Boyd and Fraser Publishing. Madwa, R. (1999). "[The Social History of Leimerr Park]"

Lasley, J. R. (1002). *Age, Social Context, and Street Gang Membership: "Youth" Gangs Becoming "Adult" Gangs?* Youth & Society, 23, (4), 434-451.

Lessons not learned from History, (1984). *Awake,* (Watchtower Bible and Trace Society), 65, pp. 4-7.

Lewis, B. (1992). Do Conduct Disordered Gang Members think Differently? Journal of Emotional and Behavioral Problems 1, p. 17-20.

Maas, P., (1968). *The Balachi Papers.* New York: G. P. Putnam's Sons.

Marin, G., Otero-Sabogai, R., Marin, G. A. & Perez-Stable, E. J. (1985). *Hispanic Families and Acculturation-What Changes and Does Not.* Hispanic Journal of Behavior Science, 2, 379-412.

McWilliams, C. (1946). *Southern California Country.* New York: American Book-Stratford Press.

McWilliams, C. (1949). *North from Mexico.* Philadelphia: J. B. Lippincott.

McWilliams, C. (1983). *Pachucos and the Zoot-suit Riots.* In L. I. Duran & H. Bernard (Eds.), *Introduction to Chicano Studies* (pp. 450-470). New York: Macmillan.

Maxson, C. L. and Klein, M. W. (1990). "Street Gang Violence: Twice as Great or Half as Great?" pp. 71-100 in Ronald Huff (ed), *Gangs in America.* New Bury Park, CA: Sage.

Miranda, K. M., (2003). *Homegirls in the Public Sphere.* Austin University of Texas Press.

Moore, J. (1978). *Homeboys: Gangs, and prison in the barrios of Los Angeles.* Philadelphia: Tempe University Press.

Moquin, W., & Van Doren, C. (1971). *A Documentary History of the Mexican Americans.* New York: Praeger.

Padilla, E. R. C., Maldonado, M. & Garcia. R. E. (1988). Coping responses to Psychological stressors among Mexican and Central-American immigrants.

Ponce, F. Q., & Atkinson, D. R. (1989). Mexican-American Acculturation, Counselor Ethnicity, Counseling Style, and Perceived Counselor Credibility. *Journal of Counseling Psychology*, 36, 203-208.

Poston, R. W. (1971). *The Gang and the Establishment*. New York: Harper & Row.

Rak, F. C., & Patterson, E. L. (1996). Promoting Resilience in At-risk Children. *Journal of Counseling and Development*, 74, 368-373.

Rodríguez, Luis. *Always Running; La Vida Loca, Gang Days in LA*, etc.

Romo, R. (1983). *East Los Angeles: History of a Barrio*. Austin: University Press of Texas.

Samora, J., & Simon, P. V. (1977). *A history of the Mexican American People*. Notre Dame Press.

Sanchez, G., *Becoming Mexican American*. NY: Oxford University Press, 1993.

Sloan, D. L. (1993). *Reasons and Remedies for Gangs and Delinquency among School Age Children*. Literature Review, ERIC No. 362603.

Silverman, C. 1994). Do You Know Where Your Children Are? *The Municipality November*, p415-418.

Smart, K. F., & Smart D. W. (1993). Acculturation, Biculturalism, and the Rehabilitation of Mexican Americans. *Journal of Applied Rehabilitation Counseling*, 24, 46-51.

Smart, J. F. M., & Smart D. W. (1994). The Rehabilitation of Hispanics-Experiencing, Acculturative Stress: Implications for Practice. *Journal of Rehabilitation*. 10, 8-12.

Sondern, F., (1959). *Brotherhood of Evil: The Mafia*. New York: Farrar, Strauss, & Cudahy.

Spergel, I. A. (1992). Youth Gangs: An Essay Review. *Social Service Review*, March 121-139. Study of Delinquent Gangs: Progress Report, (1962). Los Angeles County Probation Department and the Youth Studies Center, University of Southern California, August 31.

Taylor, E. S., Peplau, A. L., Sears, O. D. (2000). *Social Psychology*. University of California, Los Angeles, Prentice Hall, Saddle River, New Jersey.

The Civil Rights Movement to Little Africa. Senior thesis, under Professor Szelenyi, Sociology Department, University of California, Los Angeles.

Thornberry, P. (1993). The Role of Juvenile Gangs in Facilitating Delinquent Behavior *Journal of Research, Crime, & Delinquency* 30 (1) 55-87.

Thrasher, F. M. (1963). *The Gang*: (abridged ed.). Chicago: University of Chicago Press. Tolbert, E. J. (1980). *The UNIA and Black Los Angeles: Ideology and Community in the American Garvey Movement*. Los Angeles: Center for Afro-Americans Studies, University of California, Los Angeles.

U.S. Department of Commerce, Bureau of the Census. (1982). *United States Census of Population 1980: Characteristics of the Population*. Washington, DC: Government Printing Office.

Vigil, D. J., (2000). *A Rainbow of Gangs: Street Cultures in the Megacity*. University of Texas Press, Austin.

West, P. (1981, March 24). *Street Gangs Expand Numbers and Intensity*. Campus Strife, pp. 12-13.

Whyte, W.F. (1981). *Street Corner Society*. Chicago: University of Chicago Press.

Appendix A

"Set A" Questions for Non-Gang Members

"Set A" Questions for Non-Gang Members

I. Personal Information

　　1.　Your name (title, if any):

　　2.　Where do you live?

　　3.　How long have you lived here?

　　4.　What kind of work do you do? How long?

II. Gang-Related Data

　　1.　Do you happen to know when gangs began to appear in the County of Los Angeles?

　　2.　When were you first aware of theses gangs?

　　3.　Do you know about the history of Chicano/Latino gangs in Los Angeles?

　　4.　When were you first aware of these gangs?

5. What do you believe is the reason gangs have expanded?
6. Are the gang members younger today than 10, 20, 30 years ago?
7. Are they more violent than before?
8. Has there been an increase in crime by gangs?
9. Is the crime related to drug usage?
10. Do you personally work with gangs?
11. Have you dealt with gang members?
12. What do you believe is the reason that gangs fight?
13. Were gangs only Chicano/Latino in the 40s, 50s, and 60s?
14. What do you believe is the reason that gangs continue the warfare?
15. What do you believe is the reason that youth join gangs today?
16. Are there gangs in the jail/prison system?
17. Why do members join the prison gangs?
18. Are gangs here to stay?
19. Will they continue to be a threat to society?

III. Programs for Control

1. What has been to reduce gang violence?
2. What agencies have had an impact on gang?
3. How effective are they?
4. As a non-profit organization, do you work with gangs?
5. Are your services open to anyone?
6. What are the results of those who get involved in your organization?
7. How many gang members break away from the gang cycle for good?
8. What would you recommend that would help solve the gang problem in the County of Los Angeles?

Appendix B

"Set B" Questions for Gang and Retired Gang Members

"S‍ET B" Q‍UESTIONS FOR Gang and Retired Gang Members

I. Personal Information

1. Your Name:
2. Where do you live?
3. How long have you lived there?
4. Do you live with your parents, or whom?
5. Do you have any brothers and sisters?
6. Are you married?
7. So you have any children?

II. Social Information

1. Are you/were you a gang member?
2. What was/is the name of the gang you associated with?

3. When did you first notice gangs in neighborhood?
4. When did you begin your association with gangs?
5. How old were you when you became a gang member?
6. How did you become a gang member? Were you initiated?
7. Are/were any of your relatives in gangs?
8. Why did you want to join the gang?
9. Did your parents know of your gang affiliation? How did they react to it?

III. Historical Information

A. General Information

1. When did gangs first appear in Los Angeles?
2. Were gangs only Chicano/Latino?
3. Why did youth gang begin to form?
4. Why did the youth join gangs in the 1920s, 1930s, etc. (during the time that you first got involved)?
5. What activities were carried out by gangs?
6. Was there any violence or were gang's social groups?
7. Were there many gangs in the County of Los Angeles in the 40s, 50s and 60s, etc.?
8. When did the pachuco appear in Los Angeles?
9. Do you know what caused the gangs to spread throughout the county?
10. What can you give as the reason for gang warfare?
11. Why does the warfare continue?
12. When did the gangs begin to use drugs?
13. When did police officers find out that gangs were using drugs?

14. When did gangs begin to use violent weapons?
15. Do you know about the prison gangs?

B. Specific Information

1. Who started your gang?
2. When did your gang begin?
3. Why did the gang begin?
4. Does/did the gang have a leader?
5. How was the leader selected?
6. What were the activities of your leader?
7. What was the age range of the gang?
8. Was there a female gang in the neighborhood?
9. What was the age range of the female gang?
10. When did the female gangs begin?
11. What was/is the neighborhood life?

IV. Gang Related Activities

1. Was your gang a fighting gang or a social group?
2. Would you explain how gang recruited members?
3. When did your gang use violence in their activities?
4. What did the gang fight with?
5. Why did your gang fight against other gangs?
6. Did your gang get involved with drugs?
7. Do you believe that the drugs caused more violence?
8. Would you explain the method of revenge that you used?
9. How did your rivals react to your retaliation?

10. How did the parents react when their son was a victim of gang violence?
11. What did the older gang members do who no longer got involved in violent activity?
12. Did they break away completely from gang activity?
13. What happened to those remained involved?
14. As a parent do/did you encourage your children into gang activity and membership?
15. Are you still involved with gangs?
16. Did you break away completely?
17. What do you do now?
18. Why did you break away from gangs?
19. What does the gang do today?
20. What happened to the members?
21. Do you believe there is more violence among gangs today?
22. What do you believe is the reason that youth join gangs today?
23. Are more younger youth getting involved in the gangs?
24. How do you feel about youth joining gangs?
25. What would you recommend that would help solve the gang problem in the County of Los Angeles?

Article from Sun-News Newspaper
By Rebecca Johns
Sun-News Reporter

SILVER CITY—IN A MATTER of a few short weeks, first time author and Silver City native Gilbert M. Griñie's book titled "The Way Out" is scheduled to hit stores.

Griñie's book offers a comprehensive look at gangs from a historical perspective dating back to the 1920's while offering solutions to the problems that plague cities and towns across America today.

"We have an epidemic of drugs, alcohol and gangs throughout the world. It's no longer just in the big cities, it's in the small communities too," Griñie said.

Griñie holds a Bachelors of Science in Rehabilitation and a Master's of Science in Counseling from California State University in Los Angeles. He currently works as a consultant offering solutions for drug, alcohol, and gang prevention and intervention. Over the past few years, Griñie has also worked with various projects to help young people stay out of gangs and pursue a higher education including helping individuals on parole to stay focused on their education process. Griñie has a passion to help these individuals because he is proof that no matter what, anybody can change and become a productive and viable part of society.

Gilbert M. Griñie

Griñie's life started out headed down a troubled path. He entered the world March 29, 1948 born into a large family in Silver City. Early in his life, Griñie's family moved to Lordsburg but as he entered the sixth grade his family returned to Silver City where he found it difficult to fit into the community. Fear and anger plagued Griñie as he was forced to leave behind his friends and family in Lordsburg.

"I felt rejection from the community because I was an outsider," Griñie said of his return to Silver City. During his youth people in the community who knew his family stereotyped him.

"I was told to face the fact that I would never amount to anything, that I would spend my life in prison or die young," Griñie said.

During this time and despite the discouragement of most people, Griñie said local teachers Gretta Oberg and Henry Munoz and counselor Patsy Ybarra (Madrid) encouraged him to believe that he could do more with his life.

It wasn't long, however, before, at the age of 13, the lost young man found himself before a judge facing truancy charges. He ended up serving three years at the New Mexico Boys Home.

Released in 1964 at age 16 Griñie decided he was going to live in California with his older brother Tobie.

"I took off for California with the attitude of becoming a big time gangster, Griñie said. "My goal was to become a gangster because everybody told me I would never amount to anything."

While he was living in California, Griñie said his brother Tobie and a couple of gangsters from his neighborhood cautioned him against choosing the gang lifestyle.

"They told me this is not the life you want," Griñie said.

Eventually Griñie joined the military in 1968 and ended up receiving an early honorable discharge in 1969. After leaving the military Griñie was soon strung out on heroin.

"I broke my habit when I was in the county jail in L.A.," he said.

After serving time in the L.A. County jail, Griñie moved to Texas where he continued to get in trouble and ending up in and out of county jail over the next two years. Then in 1970-71 Griñie went to prison for another six years.

Griñie said as he looks back to the past, he recognizes his problem with the law was rooted in his drinking.

"Every time I drank I got the desire to break into places," he recalls.

While in prison Griñie pursued his GED and then went on to take a couple of college courses. He was released from prison in November of 1976. At this time Griñie came back to the Silver City area where he eventually met and married his wife of 31 years.

"April 7 of 1977 I met my wife," Griñie recalls with a smile. "Because of my past everybody told her not to marry me. They only gave us six months and we've been together 31-years."

Gloria Tais Griñie didn't scare easily though.

"I had never met anyone like him," Gloria said. "When we first met he told me all these stories that might have scared off somebody else but they didn't scare me off."

Gloria said she saw through the mask. "I could sense another side to him." The couple married on May 21, 1977.

Gloria recalls Gilbert's gentleness with her two children from a previous marriage.

"He would come home and help me with the children," she recalled. "I couldn't believe it."

A year after Gilbert and Gloria married, Griñie adopted Gloria's children Melissa and Ronnie. About a year later, Sonya Griñie came along.

Life wasn't easy during those first two years, though. Gilbert Griñie continued to drink until Gloria told him she would leave if he did not stop.

"He straightened out," she said smiling. Gloria said she is surprised how their life turned out because there were times that she wondered if she had made the right choice.

Griñie values his wife's strength and faithfulness.

"She was a key figure in turning my life around, she is my backbone," he said.

Early in the couple's marriage, Griñie was working in the mines. In 1978 he was injured. Unable to work, he decided to enroll in Western New Mexico University.

During his initial testing, Griñie said he was told that he really wasn't college material and perhaps he should consider pursuing a trade. He pushed on though and remembers one professor who encouraged him. Dr. Bonnie Maldonado, he said, believed in Griñie's ability to succeed.

"She told me she believed in me," Griñie said.

Griñie remained at WNMU struggling with his grades until 1980 when he eventually transferred to New Mexico State University in Las Cruces.

"I really wasn't into school at the time," Griñie said. At NMSU he received a certification in welding. He went on to work as a welder for a time, later moving on to drive truck for a living. A couple of years later Griñie moved his family to California where he continued to driving truck until 1998.

"In 1996 I decided to go to Cerritos Community College to see what I could do with my life," Griñie said.

During his time at Cerritos, Griñie's GPA dropped to a 1.5, the result of dealing with medical issues created from an accident that ended his driving career. But, Griñie didn't give up. He went to Dr. Marty Brodwin, the head of the counseling department at California State University, and convinced him to allow Griñie into the counseling program if he brought up his GPA.

"I always wanted to be a counselor," Griñie said. "As we spoke I told him I wanted to go on for a master's degree. He told me later that he thought he didn't think I could raise my GPA let alone go for a master's degree. We laugh about that now."

Griñie did go on to bring his GPA up to a 2.0 graduating with an Associates of Arts degree. Griñie then moved on to attend California State University first earning a Bachelor's degree in 2002. He eventually was awarded the Ronald McNair Scholarship in 2003 and he went on to graduate with a Master's degree in 2004.

During his years in school, Griñie said, he found he loved research and writing and as he prepared to graduate with his Master's degree in 2004, Griñie wrote his thesis. It is this thesis that evolved into the book, *The Way Out*. Griñie said he interviewed a series of individuals from various neighborhoods known for gang activity. While researching and writing the thesis, Griñie said, he realized his work should be published so he began searching for a venue through which to accomplish this task. Four years later the book cover is finished and the final editing is underway. Griñie expects to see his book on store shelves by his 60th birthday coming up on March 29.

Griñie is currently working on his second book and said he would like to move back to Grant County and help to build a better Silver City.

Currently Griñie commutes to the area from California to visit family.

Rebecca Johns can be reached at rjohns@scsun-news.com

PHOTO SECTION

PARTE SECONDA

A Touch of Hope

Do not allow your fears from pursuing your hopes.

Holding the Vision

*No one knows what the future holds,
let us keep our vision in the present.*

Leadership

A true leader is one that has learned to obey and be a commander.

Behavior & Attitudes

By becoming people of character we can prove that we are trustworthy, responsible, caring and good citizens.

Love & Support

Love will find a way. Indifference will find an excuse.

Goal Setting

Control is the connection between goals and accomplishments.

Accelerating Potential

By changing habits, attitudes, beliefs, and expectations there is no limit to potential.

www.ingramcontent.com/pod-product-compliance
Lightning Source LLC
Chambersburg PA
CBHW030326080526
44584CB00012B/728